The Remarkable Power of
Early Childhood Development

GREAT BY EIGHT

HOW TO **REALLY** MAKE AMERICA GREAT
(AND KEEP US THERE)

DR. RICK ALLEN

PERSISTENCE
ERA
PRESS

Published by Persistence Press, Tacoma, Washington
rickallenauthor.com

Edited and designed by Girl Friday Productions
www.girlfridayproductions.com

Design: Paul Barrett
Project management: Sara Spees Addicott
Editorial: Bethany Davis

Image credits: Cover, REDPIXEL.PL/Shutterstock and Rawpixel.com/Shutterstock; Titlepage, Rawpixel
.com/Shutterstock; 1, Photo 12/Alamy; 6, Rawpixel.com/Adobe; 12, Weenee/iStock; 19 (both), Gage
Skidmore; 24, National Archives; 30, fotohansel/Adobe; 38, Courtesy of the author; 36, PinClipart.com;
54, cirodelia/Adobe; 60, WavebreakmediaMicro/Adobe; 71, flint01/Vectorstock; 82, Wakr10/Adobe; 95,
Beryl Peters Collection/Alamy; 100, Luca/Adobe; 106, Igor Zakowski/123RF; 110, Everett Collection;
117, RGR Collection/Alamy; 126, ChrisGorgio/iStock; 130, Rbirchall/iStock; 136, Sergey Novikov/
Adobe; 144, Corri Seizinger/Adobe; 153, Keystone Press/Alamy; 165, Tupungato/Adobe; 169, National
Archives; 175, Pinclipart.com; 179, Anterovium/Adobe; 186, Fona/SS; 193, toonaday/Illustrations Of

ISBN (paperback): 978-1-7345959-2-5
ISBN (ebook): 978-1-7345959-3-2
Library of Congress Control Number: 2021901939

First edition

*To my amazing wife, Alvarita, who—as a truly great mom—
somehow instinctively knew how to incorporate almost everything
in this book as she reared our wonderful sons forty years ago.*

*And to Ethan and Travis, who have intuitively emulated
their mother in becoming great parents themselves.*

All three have filled my life with love and happiness.

*And finally, to my own mom, who from my earliest memories talked to me
and mentored me as if I were a fully capable adult, even as she faced so many
hardships. Every ounce of her love and affection remains with me today.*

"There comes a point where we need to stop just pulling people out of the river. We need to go upstream and find out why they're falling in."

—Archbishop Desmond Tutu, 20th-Century South African Anti-Apartheid Activist, Winner of the Nobel Peace Prize

"In early childhood you may lay the foundation of poverty or riches, industry or idleness, good or evil, by the habits to which you train your children. Teach them right habits then, and their future life is safe."

—Lydia Sigourney, 19th-Century American Poet

"It is easier to build strong children than to repair broken men."

—Frederick Douglass, 19th-Century African American Social Reformer

"If children grew up according to early indications, we should have nothing but geniuses."

—Johann Wolfgang von Goethe, 18th-Century German Writer and Statesman

"Real generosity toward the future lies in giving all to the present."

—Albert Camus, 20th-Century French Philosopher and Author, Winner of the Nobel Prize in Literature

CONTENTS

INTRODUCTION

> ## "PATIENCE, LUKE. YOU HAVE MUCH TO LEARN BEFORE YOU FACE DARTH VADER."
>
> OK, this may be just a rough paraphrase of what Yoda, the wise teacher and mentor, is trying to tell Luke in *Star Wars*. But you'll likely recall that Luke is in a hurry to fight Darth Vader because he's afraid Princess Leia will be lost to the evil empire.
> Unprepared, Luke runs off to battle—and gets his hand cut off.

For about thirty-five years now, despite the progress of excellent research on early childhood brain development, we've been sending a great many of our children off to battle unprepared.

These children's brains are not as well developed as they should be; we know the settings in which they are living have often unintentionally slowed the developmental process. And we're not even warning them of the deficiency, as Yoda had the sense to do with Luke. As they've grown up and left their homes and engaged with the world, far too many have had their figurative hands cut off, or worse.

We are failing to properly prepare millions of children, and as a result we have millions of poorly prepared adults. How do we know this? These numbers tell the story of the children we have failed:

- They are our high school dropouts (2.1 million in 2018).
- They are our prisoners (about 2.2 million in 2016, at an annual cost of more than $37,000 per prisoner). Nearly 25 percent of the incarcerated individuals on earth are in the United States, which has the worst per capita incarceration rate in the world.
- They are living in our broken-down tenement housing; languishing on our welfare rolls (50 million); sleeping homeless on our streets; or working low-paying jobs with little chance for significant advancement.
- They are employed, but many can't read well, develop lasting relationships, work collaboratively with others, or keep a job for long.

In a country as rich as ours, and with the research knowledge we now have about the important relationship of early childhood brain development to success in adulthood, this is a national disgrace.

The comparisons with other wealthy countries are stark. In a September 2020 letter, David Alexander, MD, president of Leading for Kids, laid it on the line:

> Two weeks ago, UNICEF released their *Report Card 16 Worlds of Influence: Understanding What Shapes Well-Being in Children in Rich Countries.* Based on comparable national data gathered before the global pandemic, the report includes a ranking of the world's richest countries based on children's mental and physical health as well as academic and social skill sets. The bad news in this report is that the US ranked 36th out of 38 countries overall. The good news is that we have the resources and knowledge to fix this—if we can create a culture that makes it a priority. It is a telling point that neither of our presidential candidates has a comprehensive plan for children. A country that prioritized kids would demand this of our leaders.[1]

Our lack of attention to the development of our youngest children also has us heading for a national economic disaster in terms of our social security system and worldwide competitiveness.

Put simply, children who get a good start rarely end up as part of the above statistics; children who get a poor start often do.

Of course, there are exceptions, and the brain continues to learn through later experiences. However, longitudinal studies now show that very young children in enhanced environments have dramatically more positive life outcomes as they age than their less-advantaged cohorts. If they are "ready for more" by four and "great by eight," chances are very high that they will be successful adults in their twenties.

As I'll explain in more detail shortly, our failure to stem this tide of unprepared children who become unprepared adults has America falling further and further from its previous standing as number one in the world by any number of vital measurements of success.

One of the great founders of our nation, Thomas Jefferson, had this to say about the importance of a bright and creative citizenry: "Educate and inform the whole mass of the people . . . they are the only sure reliance for the preservation of our liberty."

We are failing in that task. Basically, we all failed many of our youngest children in their early preparation. Notice I didn't say "our school system failed" or "their parents failed." We all failed.

THE WRONG BATTLEFIELD

One of our knee-jerk reactions has been to blame our schools for the failure of our children. But it is a tremendous miscalculation to primarily focus on schools. The root of the problem lies elsewhere.

We are failing our children long before they reach school. Numerous studies show that nearly half of children reaching school age are technically not ready for school, and they are likely to fall further behind as they reach adulthood.

With kindergarten and early elementary classrooms focused as much on backward (remedial) work as on forward teaching, our schools are in an untenable position from the get-go. The teacher must either slow down for the young children needing intensive one-on-one or small-group engagement (leaving the "ready" children bored and unchallenged), or teach at a faster pace for the ready kids, leaving the unready ones further behind.

And in far too many situations, the teachers are asked to do the above while being graded themselves on the academic outcomes of a largely unready class. They're trying to teach thirty kids with twenty books that are fifteen years old, paying for other supplies out of their own pockets, and working in a building with a deteriorating roof and a broken heating system, while their students are looking out the windows at unmown grass, untrimmed trees, and unkempt playgrounds. What the heck are we expecting from that scenario?

Can our schools be better? Sure. But unless we resolve the issue of millions of not-ready kids *entering* our school systems, and millions of barely engaged parents, huge problems will remain and progress will be bitterly and dangerously slow.

So if we shouldn't blame the schools, what should we focus on instead?

Better parenting, of course. But how do we get to better parenting (and better-prepared children) when we know many parents are facing extreme difficulties themselves?

As Dr. Alexander indicated, the good news is we know how to help these parents and their very young children be better prepared for success.

We also know how to help other caregivers, including grandparents and child-care workers, and in working through them position very young children to be ready for more by four; thrive by five (be ready for school); and be great by eight (achieve important third-grade reading standards on time). Some of the most recent research suggests that the earlier appropriate developmental activities occur, the more effective those efforts will be. In this case starting *early* means "at birth," and intentionally focusing on developmental growth through age three.

The bad news is, we haven't made this issue a national priority, and we continue to drift in a completely unnecessary and disheartening spiral downward.

In practice we are barely scratching the surface with early childhood development from birth through three years old, even though emerging research is reaffirming the importance of a very early start. And in addition to the millions and millions of children in vulnerable environments going without important assistance at these early ages, we have millions more languishing from ages four to five.

In short, we have millions of very young children who could be ready for more by four, thrive by five, and be great by eight, but aren't. A large number of them will become underperforming adults—impacting their own lives, your pocketbook, our national economy, and our global competitiveness.

Read on to learn how we can turn this around and truly "make America great," now and forever.

CHAPTER 1

A Personal Wake-Up Call to Early Learning

¡HOLA, RICARDO!

My mom was a teacher, and she loved her job. Having observed her in the classroom as a college student, I know her students felt and returned her love, especially the youngest ones, whom she enjoyed teaching the most. She used to say they had brains like sponges—they soaked up every bit of knowledge she could feed them.

I'd like to brag that she took that concept and turned it into SpongeBob SquarePants and became a multimillionaire, but alas, that's not how it played out. However, plenty of other good stuff came from Mom's classroom.

It was in her classroom of second graders, watching her engage with them, challenge them, that I saw my first clues to how to build successful kids very early—and how, just maybe, we can really make America great, generation after generation.

I vaguely recall Mom wanting me, as a college student, to make a presentation of some sort, to speak and interact with her kids. It's been fifty years now, so the details of my speech are foggy.

But what isn't foggy is what I saw and learned in that elementary school classroom. The experience prompted what became a career-long investigation into how people develop into successful, contributing adults.

It was early in the school year. I remember getting there a little ahead of schedule and peeking in the small rectangular window in Mom's classroom door. She was at the front of the class. I felt a sense of great pride watching her work and seeing the joy on her students' faces.

When Mom waved me in just before my appointed hour, I could feel the energy of the place. The room was abuzz with chattering children, all trying to pronounce the Spanish words Mom was teaching them. She was writing on the chalkboard as they progressed.

I watched closely for the last few minutes as Mom wrapped things up in preparation for my time. "We'll do this again mañana," she said. "Now, what does that mean?"

In something vaguely resembling unison, the class loudly responded, "We'll learn more Spanish tomorrow!"

Then came my introduction and my discussion, and I left feeling happy that the students seemed engaged and interested in what I had to say. Also, it was the first time I had seen Mom in action as a teacher up close and personal, and it was fun and fulfilling being there with her.

But I did have an overriding concern that I felt I should share with her. I opened with the good news later that evening:

"Thanks for asking me to come in and talk with your students, Mom. I really had a good time." Then I gave her my best advice. Remember when you were eighteen? You gave your parents really good advice, too, I'll bet. "But I've got to tell you, Mom, those kids are never going to learn Spanish in the second grade! I took Spanish for two years in high school, and it was my hardest class by far. I could hardly say anything after two full years. There's no way those kids are going to learn to speak it in the second grade!"

My mom came over and gave me a hug. "I'm really glad you were there. I loved having you with me in the classroom. The kids really enjoyed talking with you." She smiled her great smile and kissed me on the cheek. "Now, how much do you want to bet that they can't learn to speak Spanish?"

She was still smiling, but a little differently. As I think back over the years, several of her wise and gentle "You don't know what you're talking about" smiles come to mind.

Six weeks later, I was there in her second-grade class again. And I was floored. Just about every child in that room was speaking short Spanish sentences, and most were doing it a lot more fluently, and with a lot more confidence, than most of my classmates and I ever did as high school juniors and seniors. I couldn't believe my eyes. How could this possibly be true, that second graders could learn to speak Spanish better and more quickly than most high school students?

The work of building smart kids to become successful adults starts very, very early. Much earlier than most people seem to think, at least in the United States.

In fact, the brain is 80 percent physically developed by age three, and 90 percent developed by age five; it is also estimated that 70 to 80 percent of our most important learning happens in the earliest part of life, much of it in the first three years—before *preschool and kindergarten.*[2] Surprise! Your baby has far more neurons in his or her brain than you do! A baby's brain has nearly 100 billion neurons, and they are vital to learning. They are activated when they're connected by billions of impulses called synapses. Around the age of ten, unused neurons begin to disappear—atrophy that slowly continues through adulthood. In a sense, in our children's earliest years, we're in a race against time to help them create as many activated neurons as possible. We shall discuss this process in more detail later on, given its importance to development.

In the meantime, it's far past time that we face the music about early childhood development (ECD). Other nations are already at the dance.

For example, two of our biggest economic competitors, China and the European Union, have robust, ongoing efforts to nurture children at a very early age. Both are teaching multiple foreign languages starting as early as age three! That's just one example, and while it may sound like too much forced learning at way too young an age, science tells us that babies' brains are the most receptive to learning languages and will thrive and develop faster because of it.

Those other countries also take great care to serve their children nutritious, balanced meals, low in sugar and unhealthy carbohydrates, to keep them sharp, focused, and energetic.

We do neither of those things. We most often start foreign languages in high school, despite evidence that they should be taught much earlier (my mom was teaching Spanish to her second graders on her own). And low-cost, starch-filled meals and sugary drinks abound in many of our schools, often as money savers or even moneymakers. While these are just two examples, we're behind in many other ways. And unless we catch up quickly, we're in trouble. Deep trouble.

Focusing on childhood development from birth through age three, making sure children are ready for school at age five, and continuing that strong focus through age eight, is probably *the* base-level strategic building block for all other learning and development efforts. Whether or not we are successful at laying that foundation has a huge potential impact on our future development as a country and an economic power.

To be very clear, we are talking about development and learning that goes far beyond classroom-type instruction—the ABC's and 123's—and far beyond specific studies like math, science, music, and so on.

We are talking about physical, social, emotional, and cognitive development. Let's call it preparing a child for "whole-person performance." It's not just early learning. It's true development in multiple ways, and pays off far into adulthood.

Those who are on top of this issue will likely create the most advanced communities and economies—the most advanced countries—in the world. Those who fall behind in ECD efforts will likely fall behind in multiple other ways. And at present, the USA is falling further behind.

We appear to be dumbing down while others are smartening up. Indelicately put, yes. But true.

We will be in deep trouble because it's not only language that very young kids learn quickly. It's just about every early fundamental building block in reading and comprehension, music, science, and math, and team-building skills like cooperation, sharing, negotiation, communication, and relationship building.

Kids who are in positive learning environments very early get a giant head start to future success in school and in life.

Here's just one stark and eye-opening example: young children in developmentally enriched environments—most often happy, financially secure homes with two parents—typically have heard (and are learning through repetition) between 30 and 32 *million* more words than children of the same age in high-stress environments with adverse experiences and obviously less engagement.[3]

Even more important, at least one major study found that the significant variability in children's vocabulary at age three was strongly related to the amount of talking their parents did with them.[4] Specifically, they found that parents who used conversational speech with their children (talking about what they did and saw, and what they thought about what they did and saw—basically just conversing with their children on a regular basis) resulted in children with significantly higher vocabularies and IQs at age three than children whose parents used mainly directive speech (get this, do that, quiet down, come over here). The differences in language and IQ remained at age nine as well.[5]

A research team headed by Anne Fernald, a psychology professor at Stanford University, discovered that the language gap between rich and poor children emerges during infancy and is evident as early as eighteen months.[6]

Most of the very young children in difficult learning environments—those with high levels of adverse childhood experiences and high stress, often associated with poverty—have giant brain-building *negative* roadblocks, leading to a steep negative spiral that plays out dramatically as those children age.

Here's another startling example of inequity: about 75 percent of all incarcerated individuals in the United States are functionally illiterate. Millions of others, as we noted in our introduction, are on welfare. The collective cost of our delay in investing in very early learning is stupendous.

In the USA, some communities are far more advanced than others in developing early learning systems; these communities will likely advance more quickly over time. And the slow communities will never see the decline in competitiveness coming.

It's important to know how your community is doing. And if the answer is "Not so well" or "No one knows," there's a job to be done. "Not so well" is probably the answer for nearly every community, because relative to need, especially for children in distressed situations between birth and through age three, hardly *any* communities in the USA have a robust and successful early childhood development system.

If we successfully invest in early learning (helping to create more stable families and facilitate high engagement in a more positive environment), we are talking about better life outcomes for as many as 60 percent of our children.

That, in turn, is likely to result in better outcomes for our schools, our communities, and our economies, with the potential for dramatically reduced social costs as those children turn into contributing adults. Those children-turned-adults won't be in poverty at such high rates and therefore won't need welfare checks, rent vouchers, food assistance, and the like. Focusing intently on early childhood development is another way to fight poverty and would, with strong and steady community-based leadership, be a much more successful approach than the ones we have used for the last half century.

The moral of the true story that opened this chapter—that very young children have an astounding capability to learn complex things, such as another language—is not only possible and positive but also much more important on a wide range of national issues than we might think.

Long range, if you want taxes to come down and our economy to thrive, and for the USA to be competitive in the new global marketplace, investing in our children very early is a rock-solid strategy—and over time the least expensive one.

After we cover more of the fundamentals of why focusing on early childhood development is so important, we will get to the details of how to make it happen.

CHAPTER 2

Our Problem Is Bigger Than We Think

I BELIEVE WE JUST SCRAPED AN ICEBERG, CAPTAIN!

Children who are not ready to thrive by five (not ready for school) generally have stressful home or life situations. This is not a supposition, it is science; environmental stress actually activates hormones in the brain that literally slow its development.

The above developmental issue is often combined with low parent or caregiver engagement and a lack of positive interaction in the child's environment, which also slows brain development.

As a side note, it is exactly these two issues that caused such an uproar among those knowledgeable about early childhood development and brain development when it was found that US Immigration and Customs Enforcement (ICE) was forcibly separating very young children from their families seeking legal asylum, keeping them separated for months, and placing the children in cage-like facilities in unfamiliar settings.

This combination of high stress and low engagement, which literally slows early brain development, was being intentionally inflicted on those immigrant children by people who either didn't know or didn't care. Continued as it was, such treatment likely harmed many of those children for life.

In the United States, the factors that negatively affect early brain development are found most often in families living in or near poverty. But they are found elsewhere in our society as well, sometimes in families that are more wealthy but not healthy.

There are about 74 million children in the United States under age seventeen. About 16 million of them—or 21 percent—live in families with incomes below the federal poverty threshold, a measurement that has been shown to *dramatically underestimate* the resources families need to be strong and relatively stable and thrive. Unfortunately, that number may now be much higher, given the recent economic impact of the coronavirus.

Research shows that, on average, *families need an income of about twice the ridiculously outdated federal poverty level to cover basic expenses.* These families are in constant financial stress, which is one of the leading causes of domestic disputes.[7] As a result, while we are nowhere close to assisting those children who are "eligible" for federal Early Head Start or

Head Start or similar state-based programs per our current standards, there are millions of others whom we *should want to* qualify but currently do not. To top it off, we actually spend time and money making sure no one above the outdated poverty standard gets into these programs, when it's perfectly clear that far more children should be eligible, and that all of us would benefit if they were. These are "high return on investment" efforts that we should scale up!

The more children from lower-income / highly stressed families in those programs, the bigger the payoff to all of us in later years.

Using the above revised standard (about twice the federal poverty level), we can roughly estimate that 40 percent of American children, or 30 million, live in low-income, higher-stress, lower-engagement families. (Low engagement is typically a result of parents who grew up in an unhealthy environment themselves, and/or are currently living in or near poverty, with one or both working more than one job, or a single parent scrambling economically, without surrounding family support.) Of these 30 million children, approximately 7 million are not yet four years old. Another 3.5 million are four or five, preschool age. Another 5.25 million are six to eight, already in school.

A very large percentage of these 7 million children under four years old are developing at a slower-than-average pace and will not be ready for more by four; to succeed in school (thrive by five); or to reach their third-grade reading proficiency on time (be great by eight). They are set up to be less-than-optimal students, and less-than-optimal contributors to society over time.

As a result of the above dynamics, and with the addition of other children in more-wealthy-but-not-healthy environments, many of the pre-K, kindergarten, and first-grade classes across America are chock-full of children with delayed development.

The cat is already out of the bag.

These children are not ready for school.

They are set up to be behind before they even start, and they often constitute 50 to 60 percent of children in some kindergarten or elementary classrooms.

Most do not reach a third-grade reading level on time, because teachers aren't miracle workers and the needed reinforcement from home typically isn't present.

Poor brain development and the resulting lack of school readiness in our young children goes a long way toward explaining why the United States is no longer anywhere near number one in a very long list of important categories.

In fact, things are in such crisis that we now rank between eleventh and eighteenth among the top twenty-four industrialized nations for high school graduation rates, according to various organizations that measure such things. After World War II, we led the world in that category.

But that's not all. Take a look at *these* scary numbers:

From the late 1940s through the 1950s, the United States was first or widely perceived as first in the world among various indicators of excellence. One obvious reason is that our country was one of the few not decimated economically by World War II. We had little competition. Our estimated rankings today vary somewhat from source to source and year to year, but nearly all show the USA far from number one, indicating steep decline.

Late 1940s–1950s Ranking vs. Current Ranking

#1 Overall Education, now #14–17

#1 High School Graduation Rate, now #11–18

#1 College Graduation Rate, now #15

#1 Technical Skills, now #34

#1 Overall Happiness, now #17

#1 Freedom from Corruption, now #24

#1 Freedom of the Press, now #46

#1 Development of Critical Infrastructure, now #12

#1 Leader in Environmental Advances, now #8

#1 Overall Health Care Efficiency, now #44

#1 Overall Quality of Life, now #17

#1 National Satisfaction, now #19

#1 Raising Healthy and Successful Children, now #9

#1 Global Connectedness, now #89 of 101

#1 Least Child Poverty, now #34 of 35

N/A Gender Equality, now #23

N/A Literacy, now #24

N/A Equitable Wage Distribution, now #23

N/A Perceived Honesty, now #19
N/A Least Food Waste, now #24

However, we *do* lead the world, or are very close to leading the world, in the following areas:

#1 Citizens in Prison (2.3 million)
#2 Highest Percentage of Children Living in Poverty (behind only Romania, of 35 countries measured)
#1 Multimillionaires and Billionaires
#2 Ignorance of National Social Issues (behind only Italy)
#2 Carbon Dioxide Emissions (behind only China, which has four times our population)
#1 Oil Consumption
#1 Death by Violence (nonwarfare)
#1 Small Arms Imports
#1 Small Arms Exports
#1 Guns Per Capita
#1 Plastic Surgeons
#1 Breast Augmentations
#1 Wine Consumption
#1 Luxury Cars Purchased
#1 Overall Sporting Event Attendance
#1 Movie Attendance

Obviously, that iceberg we hit has the ship sinking.

It appears we are busy entertaining ourselves and admiring our looks in the mirror while we let other, vitally important things go unnoticed. Are we on the verge of becoming a fleetingly great nation, a historical blip? How do we reverse this disastrous failure of leadership and national fall from grace?

A cooperative report by the Lucile Packard Foundation for Children's Health and the Children's Hospital Association paints a stark picture of our *economic* future if this trend continues:

A demographic tidal wave is sweeping the U.S. The massive Baby Boom generation is aging and retiring at the same time that birth rates are declining and altering the social and economic landscape. For example, in 1970 there were 23 seniors for every 100 people of working age, but by 2030 projections show 42 seniors for every 100 workers. The country is already depending on a relatively smaller population of workers and consumers to drive the economy and generate the tax revenue supporting [. . .] Medicare and Social Security. This is a troubling trend and one forecast to continue well into the 21st Century.

This relative shortage of children means each child—regardless of gender, ethnicity, geographic residence, or economic background—is proportionately more important to our future than ever before. Beyond our moral obligation to care for children for their own sake, our future economy, our standard of living, and our place as a leader in the world demand that children become our highest priority.[8]

We won't become great by yelling more loudly, "We're number one!" when everyone but us, it seems, can see that we're not.

If we want to be a truly great nation, we must be intentional, in partnership with parents, in helping to fully develop the brain capacity of our children in their homes or caregiver environments. And we should be active in this effort before our children start school—especially very young children in disadvantaged (high-stress, low-engagement) environments, where early development is often slowed. That's where our gains will be the greatest.

We must act intentionally to help each child be ready for success when they do start school. We must give our very youngest children a better chance to be the creative, hardworking, disciplined, successful, happy students, and then adults, that will make America great, again and again and again, with each new generation.

Can we structure intentional and coordinated efforts in our communities to achieve this mission with parents' and caregivers' participation and support? It's vital that we do so with the goal of having our children ready for more by four and to thrive by five so they can be great by eight and beyond.

We must pay for this effort and sustain it—and do it while avoiding another huge bureaucracy.

A number of these goals have been reached to some degree in some communities (although key questions dangerously linger). If we come together and emulate real-life examples grounded in best practices and leading-edge research to work toward the common goal of building great community-based ECD throughout the nation, we can lead the world once again, over many generations.

Fortunately, it's not rocket science. But it is brain science.

And curiously, both Ivanka Trump and Hillary Clinton are right about the vital importance of early childhood development (as we shall discuss shortly). If we can get the Trumps and the Clintons to actually agree on something, shouldn't we all be paying a lot more attention to the issue and working on it together?

Yes, we should.

CHAPTER 3

Clinton and Trump Agree. Can't We?

MAKING EARLY CHILDHOOD DEVELOPMENT OUR FIRST PRIORITY

When Ivanka Trump proposed her plan for up to eight weeks of federally funded maternity leave, her proposal was panned by the right for creating "another disincentive for work and advancement that traps families in poverty" (that's from the *Wall Street Journal*),[9] and panned by the left for not including leave for parents regardless of sexual orientation or marital status.

Either the *Wall Street Journal* writer knew little to nothing about the relationship between early childhood development and intergenerational poverty, or they were too captured by their own politics to consider it. Given how we all seem captured by politics these days and can't see beyond our noses to do the right thing, let's go with that.

And when Ms. Trump released her book *Women Who Work*, she was again panned by the right about her family leave proposal, and panned by the left, this time for not being more vocally aggressive about supporting affordable childcare and for being out of touch with the everyday working woman.[10] I suppose when you've lived your entire life in a very rich family, that's an inevitable outcome.

But the criticism missed a vital point: Ivanka Trump's instincts about the importance of a child's early development, and the importance of the parents' role during those critical first years, are correct and supported by brain research. Her desire to help keep parent and child more closely connected during that early, formative time of child rearing is right on the mark.

Let's add these important facts: Ivanka Trump has three young children. Her job often takes her outside the home. Her husband works outside the home as well. She has dealt with issues related to finding good developmental childcare, even while acknowledging that she has not been hampered by the fiscal constraints most parents face.

Next, let's confirm that Ivanka Trump is widely acknowledged as one of the brighter members of the family, often credited with being a steadying force who has done a bit more homework and is better prepared than quite a number of the people surrounding her. In short, she appears smart and competent, even if sheltered and understandably out of touch with the realities of most of life outside of Trump Tower. And she's influential, with important potential partners in the political and corporate worlds.

Critics have identified issues with Ms. Trump's proposals, including no leave for fathers for the same important child bonding. She has acknowledged that not everything in the proposal covers everybody or every issue. But as she indicated in a *Cosmopolitan* interview, "This [proposal] is a giant leap from where we are today, which is sadly, nothing. Both sides of the aisle have been unable to agree on this issue, so I think this makes a huge advancement . . . it's critical for bonding with the child, and that was a top focus of the plan."[11]

In the same vein, Hillary Clinton's focus on children was (and continues to be) widely panned with her restatement of an old saying, "It takes a village to raise a child." Clinton is held in open contempt by many conservatives, who've made fun of her use of that statement. However, research on the best environment for rearing very young children suggests pretty clearly that on this particular issue, Clinton is right and her critics are wrong.

Like Ivanka Trump's, Hillary Clinton's instincts about the important role that parents and other caregivers play in the very early years of a child's life are right on the mark and supported by brain science.

Clinton has studied this issue in depth (a Hillary Clinton trait, as even her opponents generally admit). Therefore it was disappointing that she didn't see the bigger picture and put this at the top of her national agenda during her presidential campaign.

It's a shame Ms. Clinton didn't lead on early childhood development as a central campaign theme, if for no other reason than to use the national stage to further enlighten citizens about our vital collective role in fostering a healthy future for our nation. Instead, it was barely addressed; it was just another policy among many, lost in a long list of disparate proposals.

But early childhood development is *far* more than just another policy. It's a critical, foundational piece in "making America great."

Hillary Clinton could have provided an alternative vision for making America great again by placing a top priority on community-based ECD to lower family stress, increase family engagement, and over time help more and more children succeed in school, and then in life.

This effort could have been, and still could be, the beginning of the change that finally breaks the cycle of poverty, lowers long-term social costs, and puts our nation at a competitive advantage.

Early childhood development is an issue that cries out for leadership and articulate advocacy. It cannot, *must* not be an issue that leaders take on because it has political currency; they should take it on because it doesn't. It should be an issue not because it's politically expedient, but because it's the most cost-effective correction we can make in the long term—both the right *and* the smart thing to do. Curiously, it is probably also the least expensive option among the various approaches to ending poverty.

In the end, these two public figures with widely differing views landed at least in the same ballpark on the issue of early childhood development. It should be a signal to the rest of us that, in fact, there may be some places where we can all work together for the common good and come out with something that benefits the entire nation.

Our last national experience in which we had nearly unanimous agreement on the importance of working together for success was World War II. Every citizen made sacrifices (such as rationing, organizing scrap drives, planting victory gardens, and working overtime hours for higher production, among many others). The Korean War, the Vietnam War, and every other war after those tended to divide us, as do many social policy questions. The 1969 moon landing is a great example of how a nation can be inspired by, made proud by, and benefit from a national effort, even if shared sacrifices, such as those during World War II, were not part of the picture.

Television programs, sports, and religion once united us, but even those forces have become divisive. Our focus has moved to narrower special interests as we've gravitated into increasingly fractured subgroups where everyone's viewpoint is reinforced by others occupying the same niche.

For all the science-based reasons we should invest in early childhood development to move us forward, there's a great political reason, too. It provides us with a chance to work together on something of vital importance to the nation—rearing successful children—and on something where we have some level of agreement. That kind of "all for one, one for all" effort can be a unifier in these divided times.

Fortunately, this effort does not have to mean (and shouldn't mean) "another big government program." The most fruitful early childhood development efforts to date in the United States have succeeded thanks to a uniquely American strength: our powerful, effective, and cost-conscious networks of nonprofit, community-based service providers. We were all reminded of the passion and effectiveness of these stalwart organizations during the COVID-19 pandemic. They helped us through that disaster with their important knowledge of local conditions and resources. And with few exceptions, they provide vital assistance without the costly hovering of state and federal officials. If we give these organizations the opportunity to develop an aggressive, effective, sustainable community-centered ECD effort, based on best practices and emerging research, there is ample and very recent evidence that they can be successful.

In many communities, these nonprofits—small and underfunded as they tend to be—already work effectively with children and families. They are often assisted by public-private funding partnerships, corporate leaders, political leaders, and other stakeholders. Yes, governments (and corporations) will need to help create sustainable and scalable efforts over the long term. But on the whole, we should expect our efficient community-based nonprofit systems, with their existing infrastructures, to play a central service role. They have the know-how to work in partnership with parents, and with others in the community, to deliver locally identified priority service to achieve a common goal: healthy and successful children, for the benefit of our common future.

We'll discuss what these local systems might look like, and what actual assistance for families looks like, in later chapters, as we get into implementation. But first let's explore what early childhood development and learning means, and how it looks when it presents itself.

In the meantime, I'll wait for a call from Hillary and Ivanka to set up a meeting and see where we can take this thing. Now *that* would be eye-opening bipartisan leadership, and a great opportunity to bring us all back together.

CHAPTER 4

A Cornerstone Lesson Comes Home

THANKSGIVING DINNER

I'm sitting at the dinner table with most of my family, all of us leaning back in our chairs, trying to let the too-much-turkey-we-just-ate make its way peacefully to our stomachs. Talk has turned to the small things that indicate our interest in and care for one another. A few people get up and wander around, still participating, but using the move-around method to help the food find bottom.

One of those deciding to wander is Phoenix, my grandson. While his younger sister, Scarlett, sits in her high chair playing with the smashed remnants of her food, four-year-old Phoenix is on the floor over in the living room with his uncle Travis, my younger son. Ethan, Travis's senior by two years and Phoenix's dad, is still at the table, telling tales with the rest of us and keeping Scarlett close company.

Phoenix has his hands all over some soft, multicolored building blocks of various sizes. We've all noticed that he likes to build, even if he doesn't know quite yet what he's building. I watch from the table as Travis, who is an architect, sits down on the floor next to him.

"How would you like to build a bridge with these blocks?" Travis asks.

"OK!" Phoenix responds. His eyes grow wide as architect Travis takes the colorful blocks and constructs a small bridge, piece by piece.

"Now you try it," Travis says.

Phoenix digs in, trying to reconstruct what Travis has shown him. Without success, of course. He's four years old. The structure falls, and he tries again. It falls, he tries again.

Then Travis says, "Let me show you a trick to making this work. You have to start with a big, strong block at the bottom, to start with a strong foundation." He puts two big blocks as anchors on each end of the bridge, then builds from there, using smaller blocks as he goes, with the smallest overlapping at the very top. "Now you try it."

Right away, Phoenix reaches for the important foundational pieces, building a strong substructure with the critical supporting pieces at the very start. On the first try, he completes the bridge and it stands. It's wobbly, but it stands. He claps his hands and flashes a big smile at Uncle Travis.

Travis gives him a high five. "Good job!" he says. "What did you learn?"

I expect to hear "How to build a bridge!" Instead, four-year-old Phoenix answers in his little voice, "To build something that works, you have to start with a strong foundation." Whoa! Yes, he's a pretty smart little kid.

I know instantly that I have just witnessed something really important—several things, actually. First is the important engagement of Uncle Travis. He already knew, from family conversations and observations, about Phoenix's interest in building. He then engaged Phoenix in a playful and positive way. Low stress enhances brain receptivity.

To top it off, our four-year-old grandson grasped the bigger and most important concept: that if you want things to stand and continue standing over time, you have to start with a strong foundation.

It may seem elemental, but that idea has been difficult for some people to grasp in political and community circles. Important investments in the fundamental building blocks of early childhood development result in more successful adults, with payoffs in high levels of productivity and innovation and lower social costs. These are obvious benefits, but the payoffs are years out—and as a result, critical investments are slow to come and even harder to sustain. We are, after all (and sometimes to our own detriment) an "immediate gratification" country.

If my four-year-old grandson can grasp the concept of the importance of a strong foundation so quickly, what's preventing our local and national leaders from understanding that same concept and fully committing to, and aggressively acting on, what emerging research is now telling us?

What brain science tells us is that a strong early foundation is critical to the development of high-functioning, healthy, happy adults. And the earlier we start, the better the long-term outcomes.

In short, it suggests that some—perhaps many—of the societal dysfunctions we see now arose from circumstances years ago, when today's dysfunctional adults were still in diapers.

Conversely, brain science also suggests that many of our highest-functioning adults were well on their way to success very early. Their early learning experiences, in positive environments where they were engaged and interacting with important primary and secondary caregivers, accelerated their brain development from birth through age three, then built on that start in rapid fashion at least through age eight (third-grade reading proficiency) and likely through about age ten (when synapses that aren't "hardwired" begin to atrophy).

There are exceptions, of course, as there are in any large group. On the extremes of the statistical bell curve are those young children who slogged through tough environments and succeeded far beyond the norm, to our great admiration—and those who had exceptional beginnings but mysteriously failed, to our great consternation. But these are the rare exceptions, statistically "exceptional" at 10 percent. That's why their extraordinary stories make the news.

Interestingly, those stories about exceptional people who succeed despite very difficult circumstances lead to the often-mistaken assumption that everyone else should and could succeed if only they worked harder and made better decisions. This is akin to saying we could all be astronauts and walk on the moon if we only worked harder and made better decisions.

Well, no. Those men and women are exceptional, with exceptional qualities. That's why they are in the news. They should not be mistaken for "normal" and an example of how "anyone should be able to do it" just because we continue to see stories about them and others like them. Most of us don't possess those exceptional qualities to the degree they do.

For the vast majority of people, those more in the "norm," success most likely comes from growing up in a nurturing environment that facilitates growth in their brains and then in their best skills. Even then, most children will not become geniuses, or astronauts. But the chances are very high that they will become good at what they choose to do, graduate from high school, lead successful lives, pay taxes, contribute to their communities, help America succeed at higher levels, and save taxpayers a lot of money.

Early childhood development is key to our national success. Yet today we relegate it to "second fiddle," if that. Something else always seems more important.

Billions *in public money* are spent to build arenas to entertain adults. Heck, we even spend $170 billion in public money annually on illness caused by tobacco smoke, not to mention $500 million in subsidies once paid to help *grow* tobacco! If we made that level of investment to create stimulating developmental environments for our very youngest children, it's quite possible that we would reposition ourselves as a global leader in many of those areas where we have dramatically fallen behind.

Instead, our misplaced priorities over time have shown in our declining ability to maintain number one status in the eyes of the world.

Imagine the crowds roaring in ancient coliseums, entertained by armored gladiators. Nero fiddled while Rome burned, or so the legend goes. Is history repeating itself—another unnecessary loss of another great culture—because we're too busy entertaining ourselves to notice what's really important? Are we now unwilling to make vital sacrifices for the larger common good, such as investing more tax money so millions of children have a chance to succeed later in life, and return that investment to us as successful, tax-paying adults?

With our most vulnerable children, particularly those who are three and younger, such inattention is not just a major error. It is courting national disaster. That's got to change, and change quickly, if we are to compete in a fast-advancing world economy. As is obvious from the startling global rankings in chapter 2, we are already being left behind.

Those charts tell a story of a former number one country that now averages fifteenth to twenty-fifth in a host of categories—sometimes a little better, sometimes far worse.

Notice our standing in the world relative to early childhood development and early learning:

- **The USA is 26th in preschool participation for four-year-olds.**
- **The USA is 24th in preschool participation for three-year-olds.**
- **The USA is 22nd in the typical age that children begin early childhood education.**
- **The USA is 15th in teacher-to-child ratio in early childhood education programs.**
- **The USA is 21st in total investment in early childhood education relative to the country's wealth.**[12]

Well, well, well. Compared to the rest of the industrialized world, we rank fifteenth to twenty-sixth in early childhood development and early learning. Seems to be a pretty high correlation to our other rankings in all those areas where we used to be number one. Gee, now there's a surprise.

We should all be very concerned about this state of affairs. Every day we're wasting huge amounts of very young talent. That potential contributing adult is sitting in the high chair right in front of us. Or sitting in front of a TV or video game while their parents argue over finances or juggle several low-paying jobs, trying to make ends meet.

We must act *before* children reach preschool and kindergarten, because brain science tells us so. We now know that a very young child's capacity to learn far exceeds our earlier understanding *if* those neurons are consistently firing and connected by those synapses in a healthy way, in a positive, lower-stress environment.

Growing contributing adults, and maybe even a genius or two, requires very early planting and cultivating. Emerging research is now making clear that the earlier we help create the right environments, the better, beginning at birth. Let me re-emphasize: *beginning at birth*. And if we don't get it done when we're supposed to, we'll continue to falter as a country and mistakenly wish for the false comfort of the 1950s and early 1960s, when we had little to no competition because nearly every other industrialized country was still rebuilding from World War II.

As four-year-old Phoenix said, "To build something that works, you have to start with a strong foundation."

Perhaps it's true that "a little child shall lead them."

CHAPTER 5

A Shocking Revelation

SAFE AND SANE SETTINGS FOR BRAIN DEVELOPMENT

Recently, I was changing an outdoor spotlight that illuminates part of our home exterior at night. We live in the often-overcast Northwest, where it's dark at 4:30 p.m. in the winter. It was cold and rainy, and evening was setting in. One of my spotlights was on, but this other one was a goner. The rain quickened and it was getting darker, so I was in a hurry. Leaning down toward the ground where the light was mounted, I awkwardly unscrewed the cover lens and then began working as fast as I could to unscrew the burned-out bulb. The wind and rain were coming down harder—soaking me, the lens, the bulb, and everything else. As I began screwing the new bulb into place, the light flickered . . .

Zap! An electrical shock ran up my hand to my arm, from the wet socket and the metal outer edge of the light bulb.

Yes, it caught my attention. I was suddenly very awake and aware!

Fortunately, I wasn't hurt—the shock simply made me stumble back. But I never saw it coming. That electrical impulse somehow jumped across open space and briefly lit up my world.

Maybe you've had a similar experience. If so, you'll understand what I'm about to share regarding a baby's brain, and how the very early electrical and chemical impulses in it can light up a young child's world—but in a completely different, far more positive and important way.

As we've discussed, when a baby is born, it has billions more brain neurons and potential synapses than an adult. Synapses are connectors in the brain that send electrical-chemical impulses from one part of the brain, one neuron, to another. The impulses dart across open space to other neurons as new experiences activate them.

The baby brain is smaller in volume than the adult brain, but it grows quite rapidly in size. As it grows, the vast array of neurons are first connected by about twenty-five hundred synapses per neuron, leading and connecting to other neurons. These are the pathways through which signals are sent in the brain. Over a few years, the healthy, well-developed infant/child brain quickly develops more and more synapses through new experiences, learning, and repetition—building a messaging network through *as many as fifteen thousand synapses per neuron*. At the height of its development, a child's brain may have up to a thousand trillion synapses connecting to a hundred billion neurons.

This metaphor might be useful. Think of the brain as a sophisticated highway system. When automobiles were in their infancy, we were connected by only a few roads or bridges that enhanced our ability to get where we wanted to go. As we learned through repetition where people were traveling, we built our infrastructure accordingly, making it more rapid and permanent. Soon we were speeding along well-developed freeways, roads, and bridges all across the nation, reaching our desired destinations more quickly and confidently.

The development of our highway system roughly mirrors the development of the brain's infrastructure in a very young child. Through multiple and repeated "travel" experiences, brain infrastructure is formed and made permanent. Unused pathways later deteriorate.

Children who live in a world that facilitates the development of brain infrastructure (more and more synapses connecting more and more neurons connecting more and more of the brain) will speed along rapidly, firing on all cylinders and reaching their desired destinations more quickly. Those who live in environments that don't facilitate the rapid building of the brain's infrastructure will likely be puttering along. They're still traveling, but more slowly and less confidently on lesser-developed pathways, and falling farther and farther behind.

The brain infrastructure of children in high-stress environments will not develop at a rate anywhere near that of children in low-stress, high-engagement environments.

Even as they outwardly appear to be learning and growing (which in fact they are), their internal brain infrastructure is not being built as quickly as that of children in positive environments. Soon their cognitive "highway systems" will be outdated compared to their peers'. Those more advanced kids will be zooming along, their activated synapses connected to more neurons, their brains shifted into a higher gear.

The more of those billions of synapses that are operating at full capacity, the more potential a child has for success in later life. (Brain researchers will laugh here, because they know it's far more complicated than that. But the main point about developing synapses connecting as many neurons as possible to become "highly operational" is generally accurate.)

In a way, those billions of synaptic "zaps" hardwire billions of neuron connections over time through repeated or similar experiences. This helps grow knowledge, memory, quick response, creativity, decision-making, the ability to negotiate and cooperate, and other positive brain functions.

The brain acts not so much as a storage instrument, but as an active, constantly communicating system of linkages that grow rapidly in the right environment. We need lots of those synapses to be firing off electrical impulses from neuron to neuron—linking and hardwiring permanent pathways—to grow the capacity, the infrastructure, of a child's brain.

The reason kids *aren't* born geniuses with all those neurons—almost twice what adults have—is that unlike in a healthy, fully operating adult, relatively few of a newborn's brain synapses have been activated. They become activated, and new ones are created, through external stimulation. In most cases this happens through early positive and continuous interaction with a parent or caregiver—playing, reading, and other low-stress, high-engagement activity. This activity helps grow new synapses that help parts of the brain interconnect, bringing it closer to full capacity. Furthermore, many parts of a child's brain won't mature until later. The last to develop is the prefrontal cortex, which controls emotional impulses and decision-making. It often doesn't reach full maturity until the twenties.

If we look back at my family's Thanksgiving dinner, which I described in the previous chapter, parental engagement would include activities like Uncle Travis showing Phoenix how to build a bridge with blocks. It also would include dad Ethan firmly telling two-year-old daughter, Scarlett, in the high chair, "No, don't sling your mashed potatoes around." There are millions of ways like that to turn on a child's brain. Literally millions of them.

Constant stimulation, both repeated and new (particularly positive stimulation in a low-stress environment) wakes up more and more of the brain, especially in very young children. There are indications that cognitive development actually starts before birth (a baby in the womb responding to music, for example) and then accelerates (hopefully) after birth. In the right environment, that acceleration continues through about age ten. So, it's in these very early years, especially from birth through age three, that great contributors to society are made.

Now we understand why reading to a child very early, even before they can understand the words, is so important.

Reading isn't just about improving vocabulary and literacy—it's also about positive parental engagement. It's about looking at the pictures, and turning and feeling the pages. It's about hearing the words and seeing the print on the page at the same time. It's about seeing Mom or Dad smile, developing a trusting relationship, the fun of learning surrounded by the warmth of an adult . . . and on and on and on. It's about far more than reading, even though reading is truly an important activity. It's about positive brain stimulation, high engagement, all those millions of ways to turn on a child's brain.

And now we understand why play is so important in those very early years, even before the child can understand it all.

Play isn't just about having fun and feeling good; it's also about learning how to interact with others, how to share, how to work out disagreements, how to engage with various playthings, how to follow instructions, and how to create and explore without fear. Play, too, is about positive brain stimulation, moving toward those millions of ways to turn on the brain—shooting electrical impulses from neuron to neuron, building pathways to knowledge, creativity, and good decision-making. The extra benefit of play is that it facilitates its own low-stress, highly positive environment, which is a key to brain receptivity.

Conversely, high-stress environments that subject children to numerous adverse experiences slow brain development by inducing hormones that prevent synaptic connections between neurons. These negative environments especially include the following experiences:[13]

- **Emotional abuse**
- **Physical abuse**
- **Sexual abuse**
- **Violence against a parent (most often the mother)**
- **Household substance abuse**
- **Mental illness in household**
- **Parental separation or divorce**
- **A criminal household member**
- **Emotional neglect**
- **Physical neglect**

Research is clear that these adverse experiences are more abundant in economically distressed households, particularly with families living in poverty. That's why working with these families to reduce stress and increase positive child engagement is so important.

Research indicates that 25 to 30 percent of *all* children are overloaded with stress hormones—and that rate is even higher in urban settings and high-poverty areas.

An equal percentage of young children may be in low-engagement environments—for example, with a single parent working two jobs, and therefore unable to spend as much time with the child as they might want, even making simple (but vitally important) conversation. Low engagement also slows brain development, as there is less to stimulate the firing of synapses.

As the Packard Foundation study makes clear, "the greatest gains are made for investments in children from the most impoverished families."[14]

Very young children are often limited by gaps in parental development and availability. This is the "it takes a village part": unless others take the opportunity to help engage them, using creative, positive ways to send a different set of electrical impulses through their brains, children in these sparse environments are likely to develop more slowly.

Given how new and repeated experiences in positive settings develop the brain, it's important (for example) to get your child swimming lessons early, even if you can't swim; to get them music lessons early, or just sing children's songs with them when they are very young, even if you can't sing well, dance, or play an instrument. Sit with them and read, or get down on the floor with them and play—or carry them around the house before they can talk, and tell them the names of things anyway. Take them to a park to play with other kids. Show up when invited to children's birthday parties, so your child and others can learn through experience and brain stimulation the lessons of shared play, cooperation, and group interaction. Have conversations with your child, asking about their day. If you can afford it, send your toddler to a childcare center that understands child development and engages in positive, stimulating activities instead of parking kids in front of a TV or electronic game all day.

A child's brain is like a sponge from day one, just like Mom said in chapter 1. They soak up information, which connects new parts of the brain as they learn. New, quicker pathways develop.

They (and you, and their other caregivers) are waking up their little brains every day. They are becoming awake and aware through a series of electrical impulses that connect and activate the brain. The figurative light bulb is coming on, lighting up their world.

Not all children are so lucky. You know that. You've seen them.

I remember from my childhood a family whose young kids acted in random, illogical ways. They'd do the dumbest stuff sometimes, and I'd wonder, *What were they thinking?*

Later in life, I found out that their mom had developed mental illness when several of them were very young, and their dad juggled two jobs, often working thirteen or fourteen hours a day, including weekends, just to give them the basics of food and shelter. And the kids, who covered a wide age range, were taking care of one another.

On the one hand, this is a positive story of survival and the willingness to do what it takes to provide for a family in distress. On the other, it's a story about how circumstances can prevent children from reaching their full potential, mainly because they didn't have the early opportunity to have their little brains more fully engaged, with consistent, positive learning opportunities in a low-stress environment. And for several (not all) of them, the end result appeared to be random and often illogical behavior.

Of course, there were various dynamics at play. But given what we now know about the importance of a low-stress environment and continuous, positive parental engagement, there is little doubt that the lack of both was a major inhibitor of their development.

I'll bet you remember kids with similar families and circumstances. Families like those are the ones we must do our best to assist, because the payoff for those kids, and for society as a whole, would be tremendous. It behooves all of us to identify which families with very young kids need the most help, and to find ways to help them. For their sake as well as ours, we must help create more positive settings where many thousands more children can thrive.

BEING IN SAFE AND SANE SETTINGS

Our common goal should be to surround all our very youngest children with Stable and Formative Environments (SAFE). These are positive, low-stress settings where their brain development will thrive. Hormones released in the brain in highly stressful settings make it more difficult for synaptic impulses to fire, which is why SAFE settings are critical.

When children are in SAFE settings, their brains will more likely experience Synapse-Activated Neuron Engagement (SANE), the electrical impulses and pathways generated and built from experiential stimulation, which lights up the brain in the present and leads to the important "hardwiring" of neuron connections for the future. This is the essential process of building the infrastructure of communication and decision-making in the brain. SANE is an apt phrase, as it alludes to the development of a healthy, well-connected mind.

When our very youngest children are in SAFE and SANE surroundings, we give them the chance to become the happy, contributing adults we want them to be. And while most may not become certified geniuses, almost all will have a better chance to become more successful students and better workers, lead happier lives, and contribute more to society as a whole, especially as they move into their twenties. That, in turn, will drive our social costs down in the long term and improve our international competitiveness.

If we aren't measurably helping more families create healthy developmental environments for their newborns to three-year-olds, we're falling short—no matter how many other helpful things we are doing.

In our community efforts to advance early childhood development, it's easier to focus on how many meetings or partners we have, or how much we all learned at some conference or presentation. Those are all important things, of course. But they are *means to the end* of helping improve children's readiness for school and success as they enter adulthood.

The bottom line is, we pay the bills for those young children who don't fully develop and later don't make it. If there are a lot of them (and currently there are), it's a really big bill. The costs are huge to our schools, our economy, our safety, and our international competitiveness, as well as our individual pocketbooks in terms of taxes.

We'd be a lot smarter to do what it takes very early, at far less cost, to make sure that as few kids as possible end up as part of the ugly statistics that exist today.

CHAPTER 6

The Sustained Power of Early Learning

MEET MY NINETY-SIX-YEAR-OLD MOTHER-IN-LAW

To illustrate another critical aspect of early learning and its long-term power, let me introduce you to my ninety-six-year-old mother-in-law, Priscilla Moore. You've actually met her before. She was at that Thanksgiving dinner in chapter 4. I just didn't get all the way around the table with formal introductions.

Pris is a war bride from Great Britain. Just like in the movies, she met and married my wife's father in England during World War II. He was a search-and-rescue operations officer in the United States Army Air Corps. Just like in the movies, she met "the Bomber" (the nickname she gave him) at a USO dance, where all the American soldiers were out for a good time before bravely flying off, maybe never to return again. Most of the young women of the time wore a gardenia tucked neatly behind one ear. My wife has a black-and-white picture of Pris as a teenager with that flower in her hair (There she is, with the dark hair.); I have a similar picture—same time period, flower included—of my own mom, who was a riveter (yes, like Rosie) on the other side of the world, in the western USA.

In any event, Pris married the Bomber, and they moved to America in 1945, right after World War II. She was about twenty years old. She later established an independent career in the United States, rarely visited England over the next seventy years, and became a very successful restaurant hostess in majestic American hotels like the historic Davenport Hotel in Spokane, Washington, where she was assistant manager of the popular Matador Room in the 1960s. Later she was manager of the wildly successful Piccadilly Corner (now Shuckers) at what was then the Olympic Hotel in Seattle. During her time managing Piccadilly Corner, the room was styled after an old English pub. She was the perfect person to run the room, because of her strong accent, dry humor, and British turns-of-phrase. She still occasionally calls me "young bloke" or "cheeky monkey," just to give you an example.

Pris also did ads for a water softener company, voicing the famous line "Hey Culligan Man!" They, too, chose her because they loved her strong British accent and engaging humor.

If you're old enough to remember the song "England Swings" from the 1960s, then you know my mother-in-law. She had that kind of fun energy.

What does my ninety-six-year-old mother-in-law, Priscilla, have to do with early learning and early childhood development?

Well, she's a perfect example of the lifelong effects of early childhood brain development. Because after more than seventy years in America, during which she rarely returned to Great Britain, Priscilla Moore still has that decidedly English sense of humor and turn-of-phrase, and an accent that's still sometimes hard to decipher. I could barely understand her when I met her fifty-five years ago. She spent only twenty of her ninety-six years in England—and more than seventy in the United States—yet she still has a British accent, and a pretty thick one.

And here's why:

Children begin learning words, phrases, and accents almost immediately after being born. In fact, the bulk of language development happens in the first five years of life, when synapses are firing off left and right, building new neural pathways. (As I noted earlier, this is why it's easier for very young people to learn multiple languages.) If a child stays in the same general geographic location for about eight years, the brain literally hardwires a local accent that will probably stay with that child forever, no matter how long they live somewhere else. Remember our discussion about neurons, synapses, and hardwiring learning and memory? That's how powerful early learning is. Lifelong powerful.

We now know that the more a young child's brain synapses are activated in a positive, low-stress environment, the more they hardwire in—and the greater that child's potential for high retention rates, long-term learning, rapid decision-making, and lifetime success. That hardwiring will serve the child exceedingly well for the rest of his or her life.

And that's why kids who get a good start often stay smart. These very early years are likely when geniuses are built.

I want to stop here and quickly revisit the news that should make you nervous.

First, if kids don't get that important positive stimulation in years zero through three, when so much foundational learning occurs, they are starting behind.

Second, if they don't catch up and read at a third-grade level on time, which many won't, they are further behind. The consequences won't be quite as apparent through the teen years, but they'll begin to show measurably in adulthood.

Third, around age ten, the synapses in the brain (which respond to engagement by building neural pathways) that have *not* permanently connected (become hardwired) begin to atrophy. They basically die of neglect.

And that's bad news, because any part of the brain not "activated" before ages eight to ten won't function as well as it could have if the synapses had been firing and hardwired in from neuron to neuron. As horrendous as this sounds, the physiological disadvantage might be *very* roughly compared to people who have had part of their brain disabled by a stroke.

(Note: I'm trying to be generally accurate while describing the process in a way that's easy to understand. Your local brain surgeon knows that it isn't nearly this simple, and can provide more precise details over dinner.)

Now you know why so many teachers of young children are having a tough time. They're often teaching a class where 40 percent, 50 percent, or even more of the kids weren't ready to learn when they started school, because they weren't in Stable and Formative Environments (SAFE) and therefore have not experienced enough Synapse-Activated Neuron Engagement (SANE) activities. It's as if half the students had suffered a minor stroke! Their synapses and neurons have been slower to connect, their brains are not ready to fully function in the classroom environment, and other children are flying ahead of them.

Our teachers, especially those in pre-K, kindergarten, and the early elementary grades, are in a race against time to stimulate and activate often-neglected brains. They are, knowingly or not, engaged in activating unused synapses to connect important neurons in some kids, while trying to advance other kids who are ready and eager to move on. That they perform so many miracles under these circumstances is truly remarkable.

Let me use another real-life experience (curiously also involving England) to better articulate what happens when the brain hasn't been hardwired in, or isn't developed enough to send messages that help someone make "a good choice."

My wife, Alvarita, and I traveled with our good friends Dan and Sharon for many years. Both are bright, articulate, and funny companions. Dan was a highly respected government administrator—and you know a professional in that line of work has to have something on the ball to command that kind of respect.

Anyway, we had some great times as well as some close calls in traveling together. Some of the close calls are actually among our most favorite memories.

We always appreciated the freedom of having a car to drive around wherever we traveled, and that has included Italy, Spain, France, Mexico, and yes, even Australia and Great Britain, where they drive on the "wrong" side of the road.

On one trip, we were driving from northern to southern England, heading for our next bed-and-breakfast. Dan was driving, and I was the navigator in the front seat, to his left (where as we in the USA all know, the steering wheel is supposed to be).

Every once in a while, we would come upon a roundabout, which were much more prevalent in Europe than in the USA at the time. As you're probably aware, a roundabout is a traffic circle where everyone drives in the same direction and can take any of several different exits, depending on their ultimate destination.

In America, of course, you turn right into the circle, looking to the left for oncoming cars. But in England, you turn left into the circle, looking right for oncoming cars. When you are driving at a pretty good speed on the English motorway and come to one of these circles, and your brain has been positioned for years to think one way and you have to act in another way, disaster is always imminent.

It was imminent that day.

Dan, a smart guy, asked me, "Is traffic clear?" as he readied to enter the traffic circle. He and I both automatically looked to our left for oncoming cars. There weren't any, of course, because they'd already gone past us coming from *the right*.

Our brains didn't click in properly—they weren't trained to do so. We didn't have any hardwired synapses connected to the correct neurons to yell, "No, you idiots, you both looked the wrong way!"

Dan, in his ultimate wisdom, correctly turned left into the traffic circle. Unfortunately, neither of us looked right for oncoming traffic. As he entered the circle, he almost ran a poor little English lady right off the road. We pulled over to the side and stopped, minds racing and hearts pounding. The lady did the same, then recovered and went on her way. Her brain apparently had more experience with American drivers running British people off the road, so she recovered more quickly than we did. (That's speculation, of course.)

This analogy roughly explains what happens to children whose brains haven't built enough neural connections through synaptic impulses triggered by repeated experiences in very early childhood. Because they are not hardwired to make the right choices in unfamiliar circumstances, they make wrong choices or slower decisions without even realizing they may be running someone off the road.

Or perhaps they were exposed to negative, unhelpful experiences, rather than positive ones, in their very early years. This likely triggered stress hormones in the brain that slowed their synaptic development. When those kids are in new or unusual circumstances, it's very difficult for them to make the right choice, see the right options, quickly process data correctly, or respond effectively. Put simply, they don't have as many neurons and synaptic connectors rapidly working for them, and they will make wrong and/or slow decisions, especially in fast-moving and unusual situations. Their brain infrastructure is not complete. They have some freeways leading to nowhere, and in some cases no freeways at all. They are navigating traffic circles while driving on the wrong side of the road.

These kids aren't "dumb." They don't just "make bad choices" because they haven't been taught to do the right thing. They're not "lazy" or "entitled." Such uninformed assumptions come from those who haven't done their own homework about how brain development impacts decision-making, and about how we have institutionally helped create environments that facilitate negative brain development (more on this in a later chapter, "How did we get here?"). Lots of these kids are simply unprepared for what faces them, just as Dan and I were unprepared for negotiating British roundabouts. Our brains had not experienced this new roundabout issue enough, and our neurons and synaptic impulses weren't working for us very quickly in that unfamiliar situation.

There's another way to illustrate how a brain becomes trained and wired, and what happens when it isn't. It's not as funny as the roundabout story, but it might be even more instructive. It involves guns.

After a Dallas shooting a few years back, there were reports that at least twelve citizens were openly carrying weapons, all lawfully. As you've listened to the arguments about gun laws, you've heard the school of thought that if there are enough "good guys" with guns (as there seemed to be in this case), they will take out the "bad guy" with a gun quickly, before more people get hurt.

The premise in the above argument is that all the good, law-abiding, gun-carrying citizens will rush to confront the shooter.

But this didn't happen. Not a single one of those dozen gun-carrying "good guys" came running to the rescue, guns drawn.

Why not?

Because in an emergency (unexpected) situation, only those who have been *well and repetitively trained* to respond in live-fire situations will respond in an effective way. Everyone else's brains will go into temporary lockdown, trying to figure out what to do and how to do it. It's a form of shock, disbelief. Or confusion. Or fear. A mass shooting is a completely unusual situation for most people, which means that their brains aren't hardwired to effectively respond to it.

People like police officers and members of the military, whose "this is a live-fire gunman emergency" neurons and synapses are well connected through repetitive training or experience over time, will respond reasonably quickly and effectively; others, not so much. And the slow reaction among the less well trained is likely to happen no matter how many guns (or grenades, or whatever) those "good" citizens are carrying.

If un-brain-trained people start firing off weapons in a live-gunman experience, all hell might break loose. Many more people, not fewer, are likely to get hurt.

In order to respond successfully in a crisis, the brain must be trained not just once but repeatedly, under realistic circumstances. The military and police can closely simulate a live-gunman experience, and do so with repetition. Schools and teachers? Citizens in the street? Not so much.

Neurons and synapses must fire together to wire together, and repeated experiences are what hardwires the "right" behavior. A brain that isn't prepared in advance often doesn't make appropriate quick decisions, no matter how good a citizen or well-meaning the person is. In unusual or emergency situations, good people are very likely to freeze or panic—to get run off the road or, worse, run others off the road.

Taking a brief but important detour here, imagine guns in the hands of lightly trained or one-time-trained teachers, with a room full of young children, in the middle of an active shooter incident. To repeat: many more people, not fewer, are likely to get hurt.

As Dan and I took turns driving and went through more and more roundabouts, we eventually trained our brains and made better decisions. But each experience was a crap-shoot. For quite some time, we literally didn't know which way to turn without slowing down, thinking about it very consciously, and talking one another through the traffic circle in a manner opposite from what our brains were automatically telling us. We seemed in constant danger. Our anxiety was high. We had to slow down in order to not make the same mistake again. We had to struggle to improve our habits. Basically, we had to retrain our brains.

In the same way, kids growing up without the advantage of lots of earlier brain-developing experiences struggle to learn new things quickly. Disaster lurks around every corner. They don't automatically know which way to turn. Of course, they can and will learn; they just have to do more of it the hard way, as Dan and I did. Slowly. Tentatively. Through experience and some hard knocks. And in the meantime, they'll probably slow way down, or make some really bad choices, and maybe run some people off the road, including themselves. Just as Dan and I did.

And if they are adults when that series of slow, bad, inaccurate decisions is happening, and they have their own kids in the "car" with them, everybody better put on their seat belts, because a lot of people are going to get banged up. In the meantime, other families are racing ahead on the motorway.

Here's an obvious question: If you saw these car wrecks about to happen, and you had the power to stop them from happening and keep those kids safe, would you do it?

Of course you would.

Well then, why aren't we doing it?

Yes, keeping a kid safe is mostly the parent's job. Let's just agree to that. But if that's not happening, no matter the reason, it's a reasonable expectation that other adults nearby will help keep them safe. When we have very young children at risk of slipping through the cracks, it's our job as a community to help create positive stimulating learning opportunities that put as many of those synapses to work as possible, as early as possible. It's also to our own long-term benefit.

It only makes sense for *all of us* to want to collectively construct effective interventions that help advance our "collective" children. Regrettably, common sense seems not so common these days.

Those kids' brains must be activated and properly hardwired to serve them (and us) throughout life. As Grandma Pris has shown, those early learning experiences serve us for a lifetime, even if it's ninety or a hundred years.

But when proper brain development doesn't happen for whatever reason, the eventual costs to society—to all of us—are exceedingly high and last just as long.

One recent estimate places the payoff for smart investment in early childhood development at seventeen dollars for every one dollar invested. And as we learn more about whole-person performance later in life, the payoff appears to be getting larger. This figure includes much better work and life outcomes for the individual, far fewer social costs due to bad outcomes being averted early, and far more tax contributions from successful and contributing workers.[15]

The positives also include lower welfare costs, lower crime rates and policing and incarceration costs, and so on. Together, the benefits are substantial. Even if only half that outcome is achieved, it's just good common sense to do what it takes to help our very youngest be as prepared as they can be.

CHAPTER 7

Building Brains Early: The Key to American Greatness

GREAT SCOTT!

"If my calculations are correct, when this baby hits eighty-eight miles per hour, we're going to see some serious s***."
—Dr. Emmett Brown, *Back to the Future*

Given what we now know, shouldn't the full, healthy development of all our very youngest kids, who are in their peak learning period, be a top national priority, so they are prepared to succeed in school and go on to be successful, contributing adults?

Of course it should be. But as the statistics make clear, it isn't.

Our most widespread national effort in this regard is Early Head Start, but relative to the actual need, there are barely any children below four years old enrolled in the program. With a few exceptions, the United States is a barren wasteland for the development of children from birth through age three—the time when they need brain development the most, when they are primed to learn the best and most quickly, and when our investment in their education will generate the most abundant long-term, positive results many years later, when they're adults.

Here's how barren that landscape is: nationwide, of the 7 million children under four years old living in or near true poverty, fewer than 1 million are enrolled in Head Start programs, and fewer than 1 million are enrolled in state- or foundation-sponsored early learning programs.

There are many reasons our zero-to-three efforts are so few, including the fact that when our first effort at a national response, Head Start, was implemented in the 1960s, there was little research on the brains of very young children. It was widely thought that they were too young to learn through other than spontaneous activity, and that caring for them would be too difficult. Head Start was initially limited to four- and five-year-olds, and only those below the official (artificially low) poverty line.

Then when Early Head Start (EHS) was implemented, the initial research did not show the expected results in terms of school performance. The academic differences between EHS and non-EHS students appeared negligible after just a few years.

Much later, a review of the research methodology found that the control groups weren't as controlled as we thought: many children who were supposed to receive EHS services didn't complete them, and many control-group families not receiving services found other ways to get their children into positive developmental environments. In both cases, the service-level deviation from the plan narrowed the perceived gap between children who did and did not receive early development assistance.

Fortunately, longitudinal studies of these children continued over time; researchers unwilling to simply accept the results began to experiment with different approaches, working with both the parents and the children to determine if certain interventions were more effective than others. These programs, too, continued with longitudinal studies.

The results of those studies have gotten more and more interesting as the children turned into teenagers, then young adults, and then adults, and then transitioned into middle age. A growing body of rigorous evidence suggests that policy interventions aimed at early childhood bear fruit for decades, but those benefits begin to appear most dramatically after age twenty.

The studies all show a number of common results, which varied based on the early childhood development model used:

- While academic performance did not show significant sustained differences after a few years, graduation rates (sustaining the academic effort) were much better for those receiving ECD assistance; ECD students were also significantly more likely to enter college.
- Whole-person performance as the ECD students aged became markedly better, with outcomes such as significantly fewer teen pregnancies, far lower arrest and incarceration rates, and higher median incomes as they aged. They also displayed more self-control and self-esteem, and better parenting skills when they had children of their own.
- Now in their mid-fifties, participants in the original Perry Preschool Project, the first ECD longitudinal study of its kind, have provided more stable home lives for their children—especially boys—than those who weren't part of the Ypsilanti, Michigan, demonstration program in the 1960s.

- Their children were significantly more likely than those in the comparison group to complete high school without being suspended, to never be addicted or arrested, and to have full-time jobs or be self-employed, according to a new intergenerational analysis from Nobel Prize–winning economist James Heckman of the University of Chicago.
- The younger the child was when assistance began (at birth, for instance, compared to at four years old), the greater and longer lasting were the positive outcomes.
- The Perry Preschool return on investment is now calculated at $12.80 for every dollar invested.
- Based on recent research findings, the Abecedarian Project, another landmark longitudinal study, has projected an annual return on investment of 13.7 percent for every child/family assisted.

Wow! Given this rising tide of positive long-term evidence, we should clearly be all over this as a national priority, right?

Yes, we should be. But nope, we aren't.

As we dawdle to expand very early childhood development programs in our states and communities, consistent with the research, other nations are aggressively building successful early childhood efforts and far outpacing the USA. The results show in the charts in chapter 4, outlining America's *true* standing in most important measures.

It's up to all of us to change the current reality—to get more and more of our young children ready for school, and ready for success later in life—if we *really* want America to be great again, and great throughout the ages.

We know that it's critically important to turn on as many of those billions of synaptic connectors in the brain as possible in the very early childhood years, because those that go unused will atrophy.

The concept of atrophy, of synapses and neurons being "pruned" if not used, may partially explain why children who live in healthy environments and have more complete brain development don't continue to expand that edge all the way through K–12 school. In all children, the brain seems to kick into another gear at about age ten, and it spends the next several years pruning those synapses and neurons not already in use—a housecleaning of sorts. In essence, the brain begins going through a phase of stabilization as opposed to the earlier stage of very rapid growth (when neural pathways are created and hardwired). What appears to be an obvious difference in grades K–3 is not so obvious in high school.

Relatively new research offers another explanation why that early advantage doesn't continue to expand as rapidly as one might expect. Abigail Baird, a brain researcher at Vassar College, says that as the teenage years hit and additional hormones kick in, "you see that explosive growth and the gawkiness that comes with it on the outside during adolescence—kids suddenly shooting up with long, clumsy arms and legs. There's that same gawkiness when we're talking about the brains of those kids, too. It's not an exaggeration to say things are exploding in terms of brain growth."[16]

But what she's describing is not the same as the brain growth that comes from early learning: synapses connecting neurons. In the adolescent years, with new hormones kicking in, the brain begins to go through changes that ramp up emotion and motivation while dampening inhibition and long-term planning capability—actions somewhat akin to stepping on the gas and easing off the brakes.[17] In a sense, the brain during these years is taking another path to learning, through personal experimentation, and trial and error. Early learning is usually prompted by more controlled, other-person-instigated interaction with caregivers—sometimes positive, but in homes of high stress or low interaction, often negative.

In fact, one might surmise that in the early adult years, the learning gap between those with more neural connections and those with fewer narrows, as those who process information more slowly might take risks that faster processors may not. Learning through bumps and bruises is still learning.

Around age twenty to twenty-five, the prefrontal cortex matures to the point where one is better at applying the brakes when faced with a risky decision.[18] One could posit that this development, combined with a well-developed brain infrastructure from good early development, explains the later widening of the gap between ECD and non-ECD subjects in the longitudinal research.

After the prefrontal cortex matures, adults with ECD head starts, especially those who came from distressed families, begin showing larger and larger payoffs. In short, they become more successful adults than their counterparts who did not have good starts. And the earlier the assistance to their families began, the greater and more positive the impact as the children aged into adulthood.

Again, we can call upon the work of the Packard Foundation for Children's Health and the Children's Hospital Association to shed some light on our current efforts at providing that vital help:

> While it is imperative that all children become healthy, well-educated, thriving members of society, our current (collective) level of investment in children's health and well-being is woefully inadequate to meet this coming need. Consider:

- 60 percent of U.S. children start kindergarten without the language, math, and social-emotional skills needed to thrive.
- Barely 10 percent of the federal budget goes to children.
- The U.S. ranks *6th worst* out of 41 developed countries for childhood poverty outcomes.
- The incidence of child poverty has increased markedly since 2000.
- One in five children faces mental health challenges.[19]

Unfortunately, we know that many parents had poor developmental role models or lived in poor developmental environments themselves, especially those in economically distressed situations. Without help developing their own children to their full potential, these parents are less likely than their peers to rear ready-for-school, ready-to-succeed children. Negative past experience often fuels a negative cycle, including generational poverty.

Fortunately, we've learned a number of ways to help those parents—and they in turn can help their children and our communities be more successful.

We know, too, that even parents who had good role models are often overwhelmed by other circumstances, and as a result their young children are not getting the positive stimulation and personal parental engagement needed to develop to full capacity.

We also know from statistical data that many children are living in situations that challenge their sense of justice and equal treatment, potentially creating personal and family stress that inhibits brain development and therefore challenges their ability to advance as rapidly as others. A less safe and just environment combined with delayed brain development can be lethal.

What we all want is to have successful children, vibrant communities, and a competitive economy in which everyone has a chance to participate. That's most likely to happen when all our children are in SAFE and SANE home environments, with knowledgeable caregivers helping them in a coordinated partnership where needed.

A few weeks before writing this, I was meeting with a very impressive team collaborating on child success, and I made the above suggestion (or something quite similar). Interestingly, the feedback leapfrogged from my premise—"We have to work to get children very early into SAFE and SANE environments, and they *will* succeed at high rates"— and landed on the importance of social justice to this entire issue.

The responders, and there were several who agreed, suggested that unless we make sure our institutionalized systems treat *all* people fairly, we risk putting the children (and families) we're trying to help right back into a larger system that's full of high-stress factors and success inhibitors (such as unequal justice and institutional racism), which may trap them forever.

Any logical person who's aware of the real world would see validity in that concern. Modern technology and social media have clearly exposed issues of injustice and unequal treatment that make most of us cringe.

But as I thought about it later, it occurred to me that the above concern might send us right back to our current effort to fix every major system simultaneously—criminal justice, racial equity, poverty, housing, mental health care, nutrition, childcare, job training and placement, human resources in corporations, education, and on and on. Unfortunately, we've proven over many, many years of the War on Poverty that we don't have the resources or political will to fix all those things in a timely manner. If this is true, what is our recourse?

To me, it seems that doing the best we can to prepare our children to be the best they can be—with brains ready for more at four, to thrive by five, and be great by eight—is now paramount.

It is vital, given the existing systemic dysfunctions and biases shown in research, that we build bright children whose brains are developed to full capacity. We must facilitate their ability to think creatively, to quickly identify options, and to respond to multiple situations in effective ways. Quick "right" decisions can help them get through tense situations more safely and possibly save their lives. That's especially true for children in economically stressed families and in systems that don't have everyone on a level playing field.

Changing ingrained systems will take forever. That has been proven. Creating "ready" children can start happening tomorrow.

We must change as many of the negatives in these children's environments in whatever positive ways we can, as quickly as we can, for as long as we can. Even then, many children will be living in an environment that works against them. But if we do a good job with early childhood development in our communities, our most vulnerable children will be better prepared than ever before to overcome the host of obstacles they will face.

History tells us, and recent events have confirmed, that justice and equity are slow to move forward. As Dr. Martin Luther King Jr. said, "The arc of the moral universe is long, but it bends toward justice." While that arc is slowly bending, it's up to us to help young children and families likely to experience prejudice or other injustice become as well equipped as possible—now, in real time—to quickly, creatively, and effectively deal with such issues as they arise. As recent events have shown, their lives may depend on their ability to make the best possible decisions in charged situations.

And that is why increasing the number of children in SAFE and SANE settings must remain our most vital measurable goal.

Frankly, the same can be said of poverty. We are slow to make institutional progress; poverty also seems ingrained in the structure of our society. By focusing additional resources specifically on families with very young children, we can help those children be ready for school and successful far more quickly than we can expect to eliminate poverty throughout society.

According to a Save the Children report published in 2016, the United States is no longer number one in child prosperity.[20] Neither are we number two, three, four, five, six, seven, or eight. Those slots are held by Germany, France, Japan, Australia, Canada, the United Kingdom, South Korea, and Italy. Coming in at a shameful number nine is the United States, with Turkey, China, Russia, Argentina, and Mexico rapidly closing in. A sad state of affairs for a country that loudly proclaims, "We're number one!" at almost every turn. No. We aren't. But there is a path to that goal.

We obviously have a ways to go before we reach the required speed to be successful in this venture. But when we get up to speed, going "back to the future" might be a real possibility.

CHAPTER 8

Ellen DeGeneres and Worms Reveal the Fabulous Future

"IT IS NOT IN THE STARS TO HOLD OUR DESTINY BUT IN OURSELVES." —*JULIUS CAESAR*, WILLIAM SHAKESPEARE

I'll bet most of us can remember a time when we were inspired, encouraged, and given hope by something that knocked our socks off.

For my generation, a good example might be the "I Have a Dream" speech, which Dr. Martin Luther King Jr. delivered in 1963 from the steps of the Lincoln Memorial in Washington, DC.

Hundreds of thousands were there on the Capital Mall with him that day, stretching as far as the eye (and TV cameras) could see. Millions more were watching and listening on television and radio. Civil rights battles—some political, some fought with guns and bombs and nooses hung over tree limbs—raged in America, nearly one hundred years after the Civil War.

Yet there was a man, politically battered and bruised, fighting a recalcitrant public and an unapologetically biased political and justice system for rights long ago promised. He was in the midst of barely veiled national warfare, really. But he rose far above us all, helped us see a vision most of us could share, and raised the hope of a better and more beautiful America for millions.

I have goose bumps thinking about it as I write. Many civic leaders and scholars have called it the best speech of the twentieth century.

Inspiration is important. It can lead the way, create *aha* moments that enable a new understanding of what's possible. So, I hope you will indulge me if I lead you on a little journey to share a couple of other inspirational moments. They are far less public, but they offer just as much hope about the future of our children and our nation IF (notice the big IF) we act on what these moments tell us.

Which brings us to what I saw on Facebook.

More than 2.6 billion (yes, with a *b*) people use Facebook, and I'm one of them. Odds are, with that many users and only about 325 million people in the entire USA, you too have used Facebook. All kinds of information pops up there, as you know. I want to bring your attention to a YouTube video that was posted to Facebook a few years back. You may have missed it, and it's too important to miss.

And here's where Ellen DeGeneres and the periodic table come in.

Ellen occasionally devotes a portion of her show to the amazing things very young children have accomplished. In this case she was hosting a three-year-old, Brielle, and her mother. Brielle did most of the talking. And in a space of about five minutes, this little girl completely changed how the audience thought about the limits of early learning.

As Ellen held up cards depicting elements on the periodic table (we were all supposed to learn these in high school chemistry, but I suspect only a few of us succeeded), Brielle stunned everyone.[21]

Let me quote from an online story from November 24, 2015, written by *Today* reporter Eun Kyung Kim:

> She's just 3 years old, but young Brielle can recite the entire periodic table—and she just schooled Ellen DeGeneres on the significance of its elements.
>
> The pigtailed California cutie also knows her state capitals, as well as every country in Europe and Africa. She also can recite all of the American presidents, of whom Barack Obama is her favorite because "he was president when I was born."
>
> Asked if she can read, Brielle told DeGeneres, "No, not yet, but I'm sounding out words."
>
> DeGeneres joked that she was too.
>
> But the 3-year-old appeared on the talk show Monday mainly to show off her periodic table proficiency. Not only was she able to identify each element, she was able to explain their characteristics.
>
> She corrected DeGeneres' pronunciation of strontium, as only a 3-year-old could, and explained that phosphorous is "a chameleon" element that can burn under water.
>
> "Isn't that crazy," she said.
>
> DeGeneres, both impressed and stunned by the girl's recall ability, asked Brielle how she remembers everything she knows.
>
> "My little brain just remembers," she told her.[22]

Brielle had been studying flash cards her parents bought just seven months earlier. Her parents were obviously highly engaged; they created a fun environment for learning. In essence, they were "homeschooling" right from the start, and for Brielle it paid off.

Not every child is going to achieve at this level, of course. Brielle may be a statistical outlier, one of those children on the positive end of the bell-shaped curve we discussed earlier. But what if we collectively created an environment that gave every child a much better *chance* to achieve at this level? Would we fill our country with geniuses, or something close? And isn't that better than filling stat sheets with dropout rates and filling our jails with inmates, many of whom are functionally illiterate, and filling the air with blame cast at whatever target is convenient?

The good news is we know how to create these better environments; in later chapters we'll get into that detail. And no, this is not an unabashed advertisement for homeschooling. It is, however, an unabashed example of how very young children can succeed beyond our expectations when they're in lower-stress environments with high positive caregiver engagement.

Which takes us to our next inspirational moment, this one much closer to home. Well, my home at least.

In my job as president and CEO of United Way of Pierce County in Tacoma, Washington, I had my share of chicken dinners and lunches. When I was really lucky, I got to spend some of those lunches with very young children and people in nonprofit organizations that work with families and kids. It was at one of these events that I stumbled upon an inspirational moment I will see forever in my mind.

I was visiting an early learning center established by Tacoma Community College under the able leadership of Dr. Pamela Transue, a thoughtful, steady, brilliant leader, who was at one point board chairwoman of the American Association of Community Colleges. She is a big supporter of early learning. Her college had established an exceptional early learning site for economically distressed families, a place where many of the college's early childhood development (ECD) students observed, learned, and practiced under professional supervision. Very sophisticated, very successful—one-way-mirror observation rooms and all.

As the CEO of the local United Way, I was invited to visit the center and observe some of their innovative early learning methods.

On this particular day, I was shown the one-way-mirror observation rooms as well as other parts of the facility. However, I was most intrigued by being able to walk into the area where many excited young children, most of them ages three to five, were gathering around for a local expert's presentation on worms. Yes, those kinds of worms. The ones in the ground.

In the center of the room, there was a large, clear plastic container filled with earth . . . and filled with earthworms that the children could see burrowing their way through soil. Perhaps you remember from your childhood the ant farms in glass containers that allowed you to see the ants building and scurrying through their tunnels. This was a similar concept, minus the scurrying, given that we were witnessing worms. Nonetheless, it was, the teachers said, a captivating "visual" the children loved. Apparently, it had been brought in earlier in the week so the children could observe, ask questions, and learn themselves. The teachers had also been presenting to the kids throughout the week.

As I walked into the presentation and "worm observation area," I was introduced to the children, and many of them scrambled over to ask me if I was there to learn about the worms, too. I said yes. Then one of the teachers came over to introduce the expert, whose name was Hector. He started his presentation by addressing me directly, asking me to move over to the earthworm display, since it was clear that I was far less educated about worms than the squirrely but attentive audience of young children surrounding him.

Hector had all of us enthralled with his knowledge, and as he talked about the earthworms, children peppered him with both questions and facts they thought might help me understand better, since they'd been studying this issue for a week. Hector would say something, and often two or three different children—all ages three to five, remember—would add a fact or suggest another line of thought in an attempt to bring clarity to everyone around them.

We discussed the worm's face. When Hector pointed out that worms have no eyes and no nose, a small child in the animated group shouted, "Yes, but they have a mouth, and they can even breathe through their skin!" Hector said that was right, and he pointed out that earthworms also use their mouths to help them know where they're going in the dirt. He explained to his audience that "worms have a brain, too." Another child offered, "Yes, but it's really tiny and not like ours."

"Right," Hector said, and moved on in the presentation. He asked me to come closer to the display case, to lean down and watch the earthworms burrowing. He put his face near the glass and pointed at one. "Worms move with their muscles," he noted, clarifying that worms don't have bones like humans do. "They're searching for food, which they get right out of the soil."

At that, another of the children, most of whom were now surrounding the display case, pointed out, "And they go to the bathroom in the soil, too!" All the other kids giggled at this observation, with a few "icks" thrown in here and there. Hector even touched on the issue of sex, pointing out that a single worm is both male and female, which elicited another response from two or three children simultaneously: "They have eggs!"

There I was, with a couple of master's degrees and a doctorate, and I was being taught by a group of three- and four-year-olds, maybe with an occasional five-year-old thrown in. They were excited, they were engaged, they were helping one another learn. Their capacity seemed as boundless as their energy.

It reminded me of the time when our son Travis, not yet six, seemed to know everything there was to know about killer whales, and had his own hand-drawn pictures of different kinds of whales covering every inch of his room.

Hector was a masterful presenter to those kids. He engaged them, he shared with them, he elicited and appreciated their comments. They were tuned in to him, and he to them. He was literally a Doctor of Wormology, a title I humbly bestowed upon him after watching him lead that in-depth, somewhat off-the-cuff discussion with fifteen squirming, squealing, laughing, and listening children. All fifteen were between the ages of three and five.

That includes Hector. He was, I believe, four or five years old.

I was blown away. I had just seen the future. And the potential it held was an inspiration I'll always keep with me. I was so impressed that I later shared this story when testifying about the importance of early learning to the Washington State Legislature.

Shouldn't we be helping to ensure our bright future by making sure all our very young children have a chance to develop like Brielle and Hector (and his classmates)? It's obviously in our own long-term interest to do so.

We have to make sure all our kids have a chance at a quick start in their brain development, which will help them stay smart into the future. The future will be bright if we succeed at this on a large enough and sustained scale.

CHAPTER 9

How Early Is Too Early?

"TO EVERYTHING THERE IS A SEASON
AND A TIME FOR EVERY PURPOSE UNDER HEAVEN . . ."
—ECCLESIASTES 3:1

What brain science is telling us is that planting time is a lot earlier than we thought. If we truly intend to harvest a bumper crop of smart, confident young children, and truly intend to make America great throughout generations, then we all better help create the proper environment for their healthy growth. This isn't a "they" better do it thing, it's a "we" better do it thing.

Let's explore what professionals and research in various fields tell us about the capacity of very young children to learn complex things, while remembering that it's not just the ABC's and 123's that children can or should learn as they develop. Structured and unstructured play is equally important to social and emotional development, which is just as vital as formal education to success in the everyday world. As I noted earlier, that area of development includes good listening skills and the ability to share and cooperate, negotiate, stay on task, show flexibility, and so on.

In 2015, researchers from Pennsylvania State and Duke Universities published the results of a study in which they tracked more than seven hundred children from across the United States from kindergarten to age twenty-five. They found a significant correlation between their social skills as kindergartners and their success as adults two decades later.[23] This research reinforces the emerging research referenced earlier suggesting the younger we start work with distressed children and their parents, the bigger the long-term payoff.

The twenty-year study showed that socially competent children who could cooperate with their peers without prompting, be helpful to others and understand their feelings, and resolve problems on their own were far more likely to earn a college degree and have a full-time job by age twenty-five than those with limited social skills.

Those with limited social skills had a higher chance of getting arrested, binge drinking, and applying for public housing.

"This study shows that helping children develop social and emotional skills is one of the most important things we can do to prepare them for a healthy future," said Kristin

Schubert, program director at the Robert Wood Johnson Foundation, which funded the research. "From an early age, these skills can determine whether a child goes to college or prison, and whether they end up employed or addicted."[24]

Having reemphasized the importance of the early development of social skills, let's take a look at other skills and when they might be best learned. For example, there is this information from Cherylann Bellavia on the best ages to learn music. At the time she wrote this, Ms. Bellavia owned Discover Music in Pittsford, New York:

The other night, my husband and I were in a local restaurant. In a high chair nearby was an adorable one-year-old girl, be-bopping to the music on the PA system. Her hands were raised high, her feet were going a hundred miles an hour, and the biggest grin I'd ever seen on a child was spread from ear to ear. My heart instantly swelled, as I thought to myself, "That little one has rhythm in her bones!" At least half of my time waiting for the food was spent just watching her rock and roll.

Almost all children LOVE music! Studies have shown that music education enhances a child's comprehension abilities, helps them with math concepts, assists in the development of fine motor skills, and helps to build self-confidence. Many children with special needs have been known to excel at music even though they are unable to communicate or participate in regular structured activities.

In general, music enhances the lives of many children and adults as well . . . Studies have shown that children can actually hear music in the womb, and some seem to develop a taste for certain styles of music as a result. Age-appropriate music programs are not easy to find, and finding an instructor who keeps it interesting can be a real challenge whether in a group or individual setting.[25]

Ms. Bellavia suggests that classes for parents and babies are a great way to begin, *even with children as young as six to eight months.* These classes are usually thirty to forty minutes long, and they require active participation by the parents. Programs designed for toddlers eighteen to twenty-four months are very popular as well; these classes still require parental participation, but by this age children will start actively engaging, too. Ms. Bellavia notes that classes for three- and four-year-olds are now readily available; they integrate props, movement, and singing as well as free play with rhythm instruments.

Who knew? Music starting as early as six months! Fun classes without parents for three- and four-year-old children! Missed opportunities come very easy with that short a window.

How about learning a foreign language? Again, I'll let the experts speak. This is from a science-based report filed under Children's Health on NBCNews.com:

"The best time to learn a foreign language: Between birth and age 7."[26]

Have you missed that window? (Note: in the USA, almost all of us are missing that vital window, as almost all school districts teach foreign languages not in the first grade, but in the tenth, eleventh, and twelfth grades. Oops.)

Here, too, our timeline for teaching is not what you'll find in many other countries. Many are already teaching other languages systematically in elementary school, or even earlier. And you wonder why we are falling behind.

New research is showing just how easily children's brains enable them to become bilingual—findings that scientists hope could help the rest of us learn a new language more easily, too.

The researchers go on to write:

Each language uses a unique set of sounds. Scientists now know babies are born with the ability to distinguish all of them, but that ability starts weakening even before they start talking, by the first birthday.

The researchers offer an example: Japanese doesn't distinguish between the L and R sounds of English—*rake* and *lake* would sound the same. In the study, a seven-month-old in Tokyo and a seven-month-old in Seattle responded equally well to those different sounds. But by eleven months, the Japanese infant had lost a lot of that ability.

You're building a brain architecture that's a perfect fit for Japanese or English or French [whatever is native] or, if you're a lucky baby, a brain with two sets of neural circuits dedicated to two languages . . . or three or four.

Babies can learn two languages as fast as one. It is remarkable that babies being raised bilingual—by simply speaking to them in two languages—can learn both in the time it takes most babies to learn one. On average, monolingual and bilingual babies start talking around age 1 and can say about 50 words by 18 months.[27]

While new language learning is easiest before age seven, that ability declines markedly after puberty. And of course in America, almost all our language classes start after puberty, most often in the junior and senior years of high school. Double oops. When are we going to wake up?

Well, how about math?

This from the National Association for the Education of Young Children:

The National Council of Teachers of Mathematics (NCTM) and the National Association for the Education of Young Children (NAEYC) affirm that high-quality, challenging, and accessible mathematics education for 3- to 6-year-old children is a vital foundation for future mathematics learning.[28]

Math at three? Who'd a thunkit?

These math researchers go on to say,

In every early childhood setting, children should experience effective, research-based curriculum and teaching practices.

The opportunity is clear: Millions of young children are in childcare or other early education settings where they can have significant early mathematical experiences. Accumulating research on children's capacities and learning in the first six years of life confirms that early experiences have long-lasting outcomes.

Although our knowledge is still far from complete, we now have a fuller picture of the mathematics young children are able to acquire and the practices to promote their understanding. This knowledge, however, is not yet in the hands of most early childhood teachers in a form to effectively guide their teaching. It is not surprising then that a great many early childhood programs have a considerable distance to go to achieve high-quality mathematics education for children age three to six.[29]

And this, from the National Council of Teachers of Mathematics:

Research on children's learning in the first six years of life demonstrates the importance of early experiences in mathematics. An engaging and encouraging climate for children's early encounters with mathematics develops their confidence in their ability to understand and use mathematics. These positive experiences help children to develop dispositions such as curiosity, imagination, flexibility, inventiveness, and persistence, which contribute to their future success in and out of school (Clements & Conference Working Group, 2004).

Early childhood educators should actively introduce mathematical concepts, methods, and language through a variety of appropriate experiences and research-based teaching strategies.[30]

And then there's this about math, from the National Center for Learning Disabilities:

Watch a young child—at home or in the preschool classroom—and, over the course of a day, you'll likely be surprised at the number of ways that math is expressed, in words and in actions.

Preschoolers learn math by exploring their world.

Much attention and research has been focused on early reading over the past few decades and researchers are now catching up to learn more about early math learning and instruction. What they've learned so far is intriguing. For example, researchers have found that young children are, by nature, curious about math. They have good evidence that math becomes real to young children as they use it by talking, reasoning, playing, and doing. And, they have a better understanding of how preschoolers' early exploration of math helps them make sense of their world and what kinds of instruction and practice are needed to help them build new skills and deepen their knowledge.

One somewhat surprising research finding is that preschoolers appear to learn math concepts and operations in a much less predictable sequence than they do when learning to read . . . Early math learning, on the other hand, is more like assembling a jigsaw puzzle, with children mastering math concepts in no set sequence but still managing to assemble the complete picture over time. While there is no agreed-upon continuum for learning early math, researchers have identified areas of math learning with specific "growth points" that young children achieve as they become more skilled math learners.[31] (These findings are based on the work of the National Mathematics Advisory Panel and the Early Childhood Mathematics project of the National Academy of Sciences.)

On gauging a preschooler's grasp of math, we have this insight:

Preschoolers may learn about math through a variety of pathways, but by age 3 or 4 a child should have a good grasp of certain math concepts and be able to perform basic math operations.[32]

A good understanding of certain math concepts by three or four? That means they were learning at ages one, two, and three, right? Pretty remarkable.

Well, how about early reading? Consider this, from Lisa Guernsey, Director, Early Education Initiative at the New America Foundation:

Babies need adults to interact and converse with them, pointing out interesting things in the world and reacting to their responses.

With a strong foundation of language development, fostered by lots of playful conversation, story time and read-alouds, children will have a much easier time.

Even if babies are still in the babbling stage, they are learning a lot about language by interacting with adults who respond to the sounds they make.[33]

Notice the critical role of adults, even when the child is still at the babbling stage, in forming a strong foundation of language development.

How about science? Certainly the principles of science can't be learned at the early ages. Or can they?

Consider this, from Dr. Kate Shaw Yoshida, a science writer with dual PhDs, including one in evolutionary biology and behavior:

Preschool age may sound too early to start learning about science, but research has shown that preschoolers are intellectually and developmentally ready to understand basic scientific concepts. They are very good at interpreting patterns, and can even distinguish conclusive from inconclusive evidence.

In fact, very young children are advanced enough to already have some ideas about the way the world works. Some of these ideas are inevitably wrong, and part of teachers' jobs must be to correct these misunderstandings. For instance, most children in elementary school have incorrect beliefs about gravity and the movement of the solar system. Early education must ditch the classic concept of children as "blank slates," and work to identify and correct areas of confusion.[34]

Joshua Sneideman, an Albert Einstein Distinguished Educator fellow at the Department of Energy Office of Energy Efficiency and Renewable Energy, wrote this for the North American Association for Environmental Education:

Students are incredibly active learners at 1, 2 and 3 years old, and we can start building their foundation in STEM (Science, Technology, Engineering, Math) as soon as they enter this world.

When my daughter Mya was only 3 months old, I began allowing her to touch leaves, watch spiders, enjoy sunsets, hold sticks, listen to waterfalls and go on nature walks. Were we doing STEM at 3 months old? Yes, I truly believe so. She was investigating the natural world around her, beginning to learn about how it works by testing it with her tiny fingers, watching it change, listening to its sounds, and feeling its textures.

The research is quite clear that the best practice in early childhood education is to break away from passive instruction and allow for more play and investigation, and this kind of learning early in life builds skills and interests that serve children throughout their school years, and later in life. Lilian G. Katz, in *STEM in the Early Years*, lays out a case that the best practice for early education is to allow students to be active, engaged, and take initiative in their own learning. Long-term research also indicates that being allowed opportunities to take initiative in your own learning is not only good for STEM learning, but for overall long-term academic success.

Unfortunately, in most academic instruction, children are in a passive or receptive mode instead of a more active, or even interactive, mode. Early childhood education should tap into children's natural curiosity and give them ample opportunities to be active participants in their own learning.[35]

What are we to conclude from the overwhelming evidence over years of independent study in multiple disciplines that early learning starts much earlier than we'd imagined—beginning at birth—and is more important than we'd imagined as a foundation for a successful life?

Well, for one thing, it is incredibly consistent with the brain science that suggests that turning on the synapses that connect neurons hardwires learning into the brain. And it suggests that learning one thing facilitates learning other things. The more the brain is interconnected, it seems, the faster it can process.

In a sense, if we're concerned about our leadership on important global issues, and if we're concerned about our creative and economic competitiveness, we are now in a race with the rest of the world.

To remain globally competitive and in control of our own future, we must be building neural pathways in the brains of as many of our children as possible, as early as possible, before they reach the age of ten.

In particular, we must be very, very good at starting off strong from birth to age three, *before* preschool, as all that learning (more synapses connecting more neurons) lays the foundation for everything that comes next. If we are to lead the world, and if America is to be great again and again and again for generations to come, we must first be great at putting far more of our youngest children on the path to developing strong, healthy brains.

To be successful at this task, we must be successful at identifying, reaching, and helping families and their children who live in settings that are most detrimental to brain development—those in distress, and in low-engagement environments.

Ironically, our most vulnerable children—those experiencing the most adverse childhood experiences, which often lead to negative adult outcomes—are arguably our greatest unused asset. By creating stimulating, supportive environments for them in very early childhood, we can find and help develop the potential geniuses among them (and there are surely a few), and move the many others toward a higher level of eventual success. In that scenario, we all win.

Want to really make America great? We start with America's very young children and their families, and help these children be ready for more by four and to thrive by five (be ready for school) so they'll be great by eight (reaching third-grade reading proficiency on time). Give them the opportunity to be as good as they can be, and we are on our way. However, early childhood development absolutely needs to be a national priority. We must commit to doing the work locally, with national support.

In my junior year of college, I was having a lot of fun. I was engaged to my future wonderful wife, I was active in student government, I was writing a weekly column for our campus newspaper, I had an evening hour on the campus radio station, I was a resident assistant in my dorm, and I was pretty full of myself. Oh yeah, and I went to class on occasion.

I also played intramural sports. I had to compete on the edge to be any good, so I was constantly hurting myself. And this is where the lesson begins.

In the winter of that year, I sprained my ankle playing intramural basketball. The sprain was severe enough to keep me on crutches for six weeks. This became a problem as the winter deepened along with the snow, and the wind howled across the muddy mall (the size of two football fields) that many of us had to cross from our dorm to our classrooms.

Fortunately for me, all my fun student activities were in the student union just a short distance from my dorm. Classes were much farther away. This included my radio/TV broadcasting class with Dr. Hopf, who was a stickler when it came to students actually being in class (imagine that!) and doing the work we were supposed to do. And he knew his stuff. Everyone was intimidated by the guy, in sort of a good way.

Being a semi-big man on campus and an actual college newspaper writer, I was sure I could slide a little in my radio/TV classwork while I limped painfully around the nearby student union, laughing it up with the other semi-bigwigs. I decided not to be intimidated by Dr. Hopf, especially when the weather was so cold. I skipped lots of his classes, which were "inconveniently" located much farther away. Bottom line is, I decided to let my reputation, such as I thought it was, carry me. It didn't carry me very far. Turns out I was a legend only in my own mind. I got a well-deserved D from Dr. Hopf.

In my arrogance, I went in and complained, telling him all about my severe injury, the crutches, the snow, the muddy campus grounds, and so on. Since radio/TV was one of my minors, I thought I should make the effort to talk him up to a C. Thinking back, I find some irony in the fact that I decided to put in some effort only after class was over, and basically none while class was in session.

Dr. Hopf, of course, recognized the irony immediately. He told me I was "damn lucky to get a D" (I'm pretty sure those were his exact words; my memory is not too muddy about that). He also said that if I ever underperformed like that again, I might as well not take any more radio/TV classes.

Lesson learned. It was a lesson about doing my homework, getting stuff done, and getting it done on time. About meeting deadlines and expectations. That embarrassing experience helped me the rest of my life.

The serious question for us is this: Now that we know how important early childhood development is, and how important it is to start doing that work now because we are already falling behind, are we going to do what needs to be done?

Or are we going to make excuses, limp around, fall back on our tattered reputation, and further perpetuate really bad results?

Unfortunately, we don't have Dr. Hopf around to kick-start us. We have to do that ourselves, and pretty damn quickly. I'm here to help in that regard, with a fond and belated thanks to Dr. Hopf.

CHAPTER 10

Do the Right Thing

REAPING THE REWARDS

Now right about here is where a number of people will be saying in their heads, *Well, that's their fault—they made bad decisions*, or, *That's their parents' fault—I had nothing to do with it. They just have to suffer the consequences. And now they want me to take care of them? No way am I paying taxes for that!*

I suspect we've all heard that refrain from time to time, from some politician or some citizen lamenting the need to pay taxes. Perhaps you even thought or said it yourself.

> But I think we all agree that we want the negative consequences of "lost" children to stop, because they aren't just consequences for the individual; they add up by the billions (with a *b*) of dollars for all of us and become negative consequences for all of society. It's where a lot of our tax dollars go, and that doesn't have to be the case.

Of course, we would all prefer not having to pay the taxes that we have to pay for jails, and welfare, and food stamps, and so on. We all want the bad stuff to stop, and taxes to drop.

We should all want to help, too, because if we don't, we will become a second-rate economic power as other nations race by us—their bright children, now adults, leading them. The earlier charts exploding the "We're number one!" myth should make that very, very clear.

We are in an economic and educational war of sorts, and we aren't going to win it if we don't make some of the collective sacrifices that war requires. In short, we all need to step up.

This demands a great national reassessment of what people around the world have called the American Dream. It seems that we are in an internal struggle with the modern definition of that phrase.

Is the American Dream still about "we," or is it now simply about "me"?

Is it still about "we" the great country, creating better opportunity for all who seek it, and in doing so leading the world in positive ways? Or is it now just about "me," a place where the overriding measure of success is the attainment of personal wealth, with less concern for the old ideal of the American Dream for others?

Are we still a place where we all work to create not only a good life for ourselves, but also commit to maintaining opportunity for all who seek it? Are we still willing to make common sacrifices for the common good?

If we want positive change, and long-term national economic security, and a place among the leaders of the world, we must reaffirm our commitment to the nation of "we" through federal and local action for the common good. And that change starts with the strong foundational piece: the healthy development of our very young children.

The above being the case, in those circumstances where the children's parents, for whatever reason, are unable to provide the kind of stable and formative environments (SAFE) where synapse-activated neuron engagement (SANE) can take place, then the people to make bad stuff stop and taxes drop are . . . us!

But we (the collective *we*, all of us—the "village," so to speak) have not been aggressive in helping to develop alternative SAFE and SANE situations for those kids. Preventive action is known and possible, but we haven't made the commitment to make it happen at scale, over time. Have we talked about it? Sure. Have we taken sustained, effective, measurable action toward improvement on a national or even community-wide scale? No.

As a result of our collective *inaction*, we are costing ourselves a wagonload of money and gradually losing our economic advantages (take another look at those charts showing our national standing in the world). Meanwhile we waste time pointing fingers and placing blame . . . and getting little to nothing done to help children and families who need it most, at least not with any consistency or at large enough scale.

Our collective inattention to our very youngest children and their early brain development has directly resulted in many, if not all, of the following negative consequences:

- Millions of American children are not ready for kindergarten.
- They don't reach third-grade reading proficiency on time.
- They take an inordinate amount of teacher time and focus, slowing the progress of kids who are ready to learn.
- They don't read well.
- They don't have well-developed vocabularies.
- They often don't have good social or relationship skills.
- They drop out of school in stunning numbers.

- They aren't very good workers, so they can't get or keep good jobs.
- They continue learning, but slowly, tentatively, through trial and error—errors that cost us all a lot of money.
- They have substance abuse problems and often have more health problems than their peers, and we pay for it.
- They end up in jail or homeless at much higher rates, and we pay for it.
- They end up on welfare in larger numbers, and we pay for it.
- They have kids, aren't good role models, are economically challenged, and live in high-stress environments, and that scenario repeats—and again we pay for it.
- Our social costs increase and so our taxes increase.
- Our global standing continues to decline.

All these lost battles don't just impact the children. We all carry the cost.

They had a bad start and, as a result, often a bad finish. They make unfortunate decisions because they often don't process information as quickly or recognize opportunity as easily as others. (Like Dan and me in England, they are struggling to navigate the confusing roundabouts, trying to learn but running themselves and others off the road.)

But if we know that this is true and do nothing about it, who's really the "dumb" one? We ought to all go back and look in the mirror.

So let's consider another scenario:

I broke down and bought a lottery ticket when the Powerball jackpot reached $1.5 billion. Normally, I wouldn't and don't buy lottery tickets. The odds are too bad. But honestly, dropping twenty bucks to "possibly, potentially, just maybe if I'm really lucky" win that much money was worth the dreaming for a few days. Why let everyone else dream, when I could, too? Given how long the ticket lines were, you might have been standing there with me.

I didn't win. I'm pretty certain you didn't, either, or you'd be on some exotic vacation on your yacht instead of reading this book.

If the rest of America is anything like you and me, they've likely daydreamed about winning big on the lottery, too. Winning millions (or in my *really* hopeful scenario, $1.5 billion). Paying off all their debt. Buying that new car, or buying that classic car at the Barrett-Jackson auto auction. Paying off their mortgage. Helping out a few loved ones who could use a boost. Helping their favorite charitable cause. Retiring in luxury. Traveling the world—and in first class, no less. If only . . . What a dream!

Now let's take that "winning the lottery" idea and run in a different direction with it. It's time to wake up from that dream and take advantage of another potential lottery win with much better odds.

What if we could all help the nation win the lottery, and we suddenly had millions more young adults graduating from school, working at successful careers? And millions more helping save social security or pay down the national debt? And millions more off welfare, and hundreds of thousands avoiding trouble with the law, and staying healthy, and dropping our national unemployment and social services and health care costs by billions of dollars every single year?

The big difference between the two scenarios above (you or I winning the $1.5 billion lottery versus the nation winning the lottery) is that *you or I* winning the lottery depends on pure luck and is therefore highly unlikely.

But *the nation* winning the lottery depends on us acting on scientific knowledge we already have about the importance of early childhood development, and using community-based resources we already have to implement the effort.

No luck involved. Just smart, aggressive, nonprofit, community-based professional preventive action in partnership with parents and sustained, collaborative investment from multiple sources.

This is how we can build the opportunity for more geniuses in our country, and surely many more young children better prepared to lead us in the future.

Of course, success does depend on parents, and local and national leaders, and non-profit and for-profit corporate leaders, and the heads of large and influential charitable foundations and similar organizations paying attention to and collectively and consistently supporting early childhood brain science. And they must pay attention to what we already know about children in distressed environments, where brain development is under constant threat.

Then success depends on devising smart early learning efforts consistent with existing knowledge, and knowing which great assets already exist (and how best to leverage them) in most of our communities. Then we must commit to a long-term collective effort—community based and funded and sustained at scale over generations.

If our national and local leaders and the leaders of influential charitable foundations *do* challenge others to pay attention and jump on board, together we can provide long-term support for local efforts that put what we know about early childhood brain science into sustained action. When we reach critical mass, our nation wins the lottery.

Let's talk real dollars just for a moment, to put this "the nation wins the lottery" business into proper perspective.

Fact: as noted earlier, about 75 percent of incarcerated people in the USA are functionally illiterate. And the USA incarcerates more people than any other nation on earth, more than 2 million at last count.

How much do you think *that* costs us?

Answer:

- We collectively spend about $80 billion (yes, with a *b*) a year incarcerating federal criminals.

And:

- We collectively spend about $300 billion a year on family and child welfare.
- We collectively spend about $100 billion a year on housing for those in economic distress.
- We collectively spend about $25 billion a year combating drug abuse.
- We collectively spend about $6 billion a year on the health-related costs of domestic violence.

Therefore:

- We collectively spend about $511 billion dollars *a year* on those issues alone. (And there's far more to count—for example, the health care costs of systemic problems like high stress and poor nutrition.)

Meanwhile we know that 15 to 16 million US children live in "official" poverty, an environment that by definition entails high risk of many adverse childhood experiences and delayed development. Remember, high-stress environments inhibit early brain development. These children do not live in SAFE and SANE settings. Another 12 to 13 million live on the edge of poverty, and another few million live in wealthy-but-not-healthy environments.

Without our collective intervention, many of these children are going to end up contributing to the costs listed in the bullet points above. We would be totally silly to not invest to change this outcome, for our own economic benefit as well as theirs. We are talking about half a trillion dollars (yes, with a *t*) per year, for goodness' sake!

Every year now, millions of students drop out of school somewhere between first grade and twelfth grade. Most of those, unfortunately, started out in the group of millions who live in "official" poverty or are among the estimated 10 to 12 million children living in paycheck-to-paycheck families, those struggling right above the poverty line. We would be totally silly to not invest to change this horrible and costly outcome, for our own economic benefit as well as theirs.

In the meantime, in normal economic conditions, we have 3 to 4 million American jobs going unfilled because employers can't find qualified candidates. About 150,000 are high-paying tech jobs; about 500,000 are manufacturing jobs. Again, we would be totally silly to not invest to change this outcome, for our own economic benefit as well as the country's.

Let's say that as a result of our work to have more very young children prepared for school, and then reach third-grade reading proficiency on time, we cut the above list of costs by "only" a very conservative 10 percent. Well, let's see . . . that's *a savings to all of us of $51.1 billion per year!*

More realistically, let's say we help more children reach closer to their potential, at about 30 percent. That's *a savings of $153.3 billion a year.*

And how about if we really hit the lottery and win big, working effectively with 50 percent of those kids and their families? That's *a savings to all of us of $255.5 billion. Per year!* If my math is right, that cuts $2.5 TRILLION (yes, those are capital letters, starting with a big *T*) off our national debt in ten years.

Now let's really dream and go back to Dr. Emmett Brown from *Back to the Future*, who introduced chapter 7 by suggesting that we'd see something really special if we hit eighty-eight miles per hour. Let's transition that idea to successfully helping 88 percent of all kids in danger of being left behind. *That saves us all $450 billion a year.* Yes, $4.5 TRILLION lopped off the national debt in ten years.

Think it might be worth a national effort?

If you think this is pie in the sky, recent research proves you wrong. In a study entitled "Early Social-Emotional Functioning and Public Health," researchers Jones, Greenberg, and Crowley found this astounding result:

> Overall, in a 20-year study, the researchers found that *a higher rating for social competency as a kindergartener* was significantly associated in a very positive way with all five of the outcome domains studied.

> For every one-point increase in a kindergarten student's social competency (a measure of kindergarten readiness) score, he or she was twice as likely to graduate from college and 46 percent more likely to have a full-time job by the age of 25.
>
> For every one-point decrease in the child's score, he or she had a 67 percent higher chance of having been arrested and an 82 percent higher chance of being in or on a waiting list for public housing at age 25.[36]

Jones and colleagues analyzed data collected from more than seven hundred students who were participating in the Fast Track Project, a study conducted by four universities—Penn State, Duke University, Vanderbilt University, and the University of Washington.

The project was a prevention program for children at high risk for long-term behavioral problems. The individuals studied for this research were part of the control group and did not receive any preventive services. Overall, the sample was representative of children living in lower socioeconomic-status neighborhoods.

Kindergarten teachers rated the students on eight items, using a five-point scale to assess how each child interacted socially with other children. Items included statements such as "Is helpful to others," "Shares materials," and "Resolves peer problems on own."

The researchers compared the teachers' assessments to the students' outcomes in five areas during late adolescence through age twenty-five, including

- education and employment,
- public assistance,
- criminal activity,
- substance abuse,
- and mental health.

Jones and colleagues reported their results online and will be doing so in a future issue of the *American Journal of Public Health*.

The Fast Track Project and data from other research suggests it's as simple as this:

If we, as a nation, help parents and other primary caregivers become their children's first, best, and most important teachers long before those children reach preschool and kindergarten, we are likely to achieve some or all of the following goals:

- reduce stress in family environments, facilitating brain development in their children

- increase positive parent-child engagement, which will further facilitate the children's brain development, including social-emotional development
- improve our school environments, especially in those critical early grades, further facilitating brain development
- increase our high school graduation rates
- strengthen our families and communities
- increase the number of qualified workers for our businesses
- lower our poverty rate, and end the cycle of poverty for many families
- reduce our national welfare and other social costs, including homelessness
- go a long way toward winning the worldwide economic competition

Maybe I'm missing something, but all those seem like very good goals worth pursuing, and not halfheartedly. I suspect most of us would agree on that.

If we *don't* act . . . we stay in the same national rut that we've been in for years now and that everyone spends lip-service time lamenting.

Please, haven't we had enough of that? Isn't it time for some long-term strategies and better solutions?

What's unfortunate is that we know why bad things impact our kids' development, because good brain and social research tells us.

And we know how to reverse the negative outcomes, because brain research tells us that, too.

But amazingly, we haven't taken the collective steps necessary to reverse these predictable negative outcomes. We haven't fully committed to changing this national crisis.

Here's another way to make the point about missing the point of the importance of early engagement and mentoring, as expressed through an experience I recently had in a well-appointed restaurant. No *Star Wars* light-saber fights involved. But a Dark Force was there nonetheless.

Alvarita and I were with friends, out for dinner after work. We were seated at a table for four near the center of the room. Each of us could see across the room from a different angle. I happened to be across from another table for four that was temporarily empty but then filled by a young family: a professional-looking mom and dad, both still dressed in business attire, and their son, who appeared to be five or six years old.

The boy was deeply engaged with his handheld electronic game, barely looking up.

As our dinner was ordered, delivered, and eaten in unhurried comfort with our friends, I couldn't help but notice the family across from me as they went through the same process. The mom and dad were engaged in conversation, but the boy was still deep in his portable game. I saw the parents order, including for their young child, without asking him a thing. When their food was delivered a bit later, the parents continued their two-way conversation.

The child continued playing his game, barely pausing when the waiter set his plate in front of him.

Now I was curious, almost alarmed, as the parents still had not said one word to the child since they'd been seated fifteen to twenty minutes earlier. In fact they'd barely looked at him. So I paid more and more attention, wondering when the parent-child connection would happen.

It never did. For probably forty-five minutes at the dinner table, the parents never said one word to the child.

The first words these apparently busy parents uttered to their child was, "Come on, we're going now," as they got up to leave.

Yoda, wise teacher and mentor, they were not. In fact, thinking back, I can almost hear the swish of Darth Vader's black cape as the parents spun and headed for the exit. I can almost hear his ominous words, "Luke, I am your father." And in this disturbing case, maybe "mother" too.

To some people, this lack of parental engagement may seem just curious and inconsequential. But to those who've been involved in the research of how and when children learn, and from whom they best learn, this scenario is closer to monumentally disastrous. It can often result in the "wealthy but not healthy" environment I referred to earlier.

Scenes like the one above are endemic in America, in a host of ways far beyond the dinner table. The reasons for lack of engagement may vary, but the outcomes are negative, nonetheless. Too many of our very youngest children are on their own. They have little mentoring in their very early years, no Yoda to guide them, poor stable and formative environments (SAFE), and far fewer synapse-activated neuron engagement (SANE) opportunities—those experiences that cause the brain to send electrical impulses between neurons and hardwire in early learning. These children have no "keeper of the Force" to help them obtain and master and use the full power of their brains.

We are building fewer and fewer Jedi warriors who can be victorious in life's various battles. And in our most distressed families, children are often disconnected very early, subjected to adverse childhood experiences before they even start school. And that bad start for each child ripples through the classroom a few years later, especially if the room is filled with multiple kids who aren't ready to be there either (as it often is). And the negative force continues rippling out from there—into schools, into the workplace, into our social service and public safety systems, and into our entire economy.

Are we the incubators of our own evil empire, letting known solutions pass us by?

For many children, especially those in adverse circumstances, help must come from more than their overwhelmed, and sometimes unprepared, parents. If help doesn't come from the rest of us, we will all carry the cost for generations to come.

Look around. We are carrying the cost now. And as the numbers above show, the costs are staggering.

May the Force be with us as we take on this monumentally important task and move forward to save our place in the universe.

CHAPTER II

How the Heck Did We Get Here?

"FOR THE TIMES THEY ARE A-CHANGIN . . ."
—BOB DYLAN

UNINTENDED CONSEQUENCES

How and when did we become so preoccupied with our work and careers and financial success and personal entertainment that we sacrificed our children?

Or conversely, and as is more often the case, how did we become so overwhelmed with our struggles just to survive, to make ends meet, that we sacrificed critically important developmental time with our very youngest children?

Let us count the ways. Or some of them, at least.

Curiously, much of what we are experiencing today as negatives for our children had their beginnings in positive cultural shifts. But as we look back now with more perspective, each major positive development appears to have had a second, darker, not so obvious side, with some serious unintended consequences for our families and children.

We may be experiencing death by a thousand cuts—each inconsequential as a single wound, but collectively fatal. And many of them self-inflicted.

Let's take a look at some of these major developments and shifts in our culture over the past seventy-five to eighty years. And now, in retrospect, let's analyze how they may have negatively impacted families and children, although when implemented they were hailed as having almost entirely positive benefits. Many of the unintended consequences impact all families to some degree, but challenge those in or near poverty even more. A few of these cultural shifts, as we'll see, also placed particular burdens on minority families, most often African American or Hispanic/Latinx.

These cultural shifts were precipitated by many of the following events, which most of us would consider positive:

- the United States helping win World War II in the 1940s
- more women and minorities in the workforce, facilitated in large part by WWII
- a lack of worldwide competition following WWII, which increased our manufacturing dominance and helped America become the world's leading economic power from 1945 to 1965
- America's worldwide image as a place of opportunity, which increased immigration
- the advent of coast-to-coast television in 1947
- the development of children's programming on television
- the building of a coast-to-coast interstate system in the 1950s and 1960s
- the rapid development of frozen foods and fast foods in the 1950s and 1960s
- the rebuilding of world economies after WWII, from the 1950s through the mid-1960s
- the new, widespread availability of credit and credit cards to ordinary Americans in the 1960s and 1970s
- the election of President Ronald Reagan, who introduced deficit spending as a positive thing in the 1980s
- widespread acceptance of the idea that whatever was good for corporations and capitalism was good for all Americans—that a "rising tide would lift all boats" and that huge corporate profits would "trickle down" to the rest of us, leading to an emphasis on (of course) huge corporate profits
- widespread computerization, development of the internet, the use of smart phones, and other technological advances in the 1980s and beyond

Let's take a look at each of the above developments in a little more depth, factoring in impact on families over time.

Following World War II, from the late 1940s through the 1950s and into the 1960s, America led the world in many things. Our education, manufacturing, transportation, and communication systems and our water, power, and other utilities were admired around the globe. Unlike the infrastructure in most other countries, our infrastructure had not been destroyed or badly damaged. And we had abundant natural resources. Much of America—at least older white America—thinks of these as the great years. They are likely the inspiration for a nostalgic vision that sparked the political phrase Make America Great Again.

So perhaps our quick analysis should start here, near World War II, which changed the face of America in many positive ways, but not without some unexpected consequences.

The war effort in particular hastened the exodus from close-knit rural America and small towns to large cities where manufacturing was booming to meet military requirements. Women and minorities, in particular, began entering the workforce in far greater numbers than before, a positive development in itself.

But here is where we can now identify, in context, some unintended downsides lurking in the shadows for families and their children—places where things went askew.

We now know indisputably that while lower-income Americans were better able to travel in search of better jobs, they still tended to be limited to living in distressed and often geographically isolated housing areas. That was true before and after the war, particularly for American minorities, who were forced into certain locations by discriminatory practices. Their circumstances were made even more difficult because they were now separated from their extended families.

Discriminatory mortgage lending, a common practice in banks across the United States for more than a hundred years, came to be called "redlining" in the financial industries. Minorities were often not offered loans on homes outside of certain low-income areas that were outlined on maps of almost every American city. Minorities, especially African Americans, were "kept in their place" through this more sophisticated type of discrimination.

This is a perfect example of an institutionalized practice of which most whites were probably unaware, never having been denied a mortgage based on a home's location. A black person being stopped by police simply for driving in a white neighborhood—an experience with no equivalent for white people in the United States—also resulted in different understandings of what justice and fairness in our country were all about. Hence a racial divide was enhanced by this (and many other) institutionalized discriminatory practices. And this was happening at a time when we had just fought a world war to protect the American values of liberty, justice, and freedom for all.

Many minority children were forced by redlining to live for decade after decade after decade in low-income, high-stress urban environments, with segregated, poorly funded, less-than-equal schools, most with no preschool or kindergarten programs of any kind. Many of these "forced communities" had limited opportunities for child stimulation and growth outside the immediate nuclear family, as the residents were now separated from their extended families and also far away from their former communities, which were smaller and closer knit.

Meanwhile the parents of those minority children were not offered promotions, received less pay, were denied entry to higher-level education, and couldn't take advantage of opportunities the vast majority of white Americans experienced every day. And if minorities ran into legal trouble, the consequences tended to be dire. (Research is clear that minorities were and still are arrested more often than whites in similar situations. Their bails are set higher, they are prosecuted more often, and they are given longer sentences than whites for the same crime. The disparities are evident in both African American/Black and Hispanic/Latinx populations as compared to whites in the USA.)

As a result of these cascading factors, a great number of young minority children found themselves separated from their extended families and therefore had a high likelihood of exposure to adverse childhood experiences. They were living in or on the edge of poverty, in high-stress environments that were less physically safe and less likely to provide positive, stimulating early learning opportunities.

Generation after generation after generation were stymied in their ability to move out and move up in the "land of the free." This relegated many of our minority children (and their children and grandchildren) to less positive and stimulating formative environments. As we now know, that has a huge cost in terms of early childhood development, and it can and often does diminish adult success.

By our own discriminatory actions, we created family environments for many of our minority children that resulted in their slower development and unfortunately facilitated negative life outcomes. We, as an uninformed and/or unconcerned citizenry, helped create a self-fulfilling negative prophesy.

We see the results even today. The poverty rate among African American families, who were systematically and institutionally discriminated against in nearly every way for more than one hundred years after the Civil War, is now about 38 percent.[37] (Latinos comprise about 23 percent of all American children, but nearly 40 percent of America's poor children.) Then we blamed their struggles to "get ahead" on them, and some of us continue to do that.

Well done, America.

Yes, that's sarcasm.

Much of this damage was happening at a time when America was easily the most advanced and prosperous country in the world. America post–World War II was, in fact, "great" economically for much of (but certainly not all of) the majority population. Realistically, however, that was due in large measure to the fact that unlike all of Europe, Great Britain, the former USSR, Japan, China, and most of North Africa, the USA was still fully intact. In fact, US manufacturing had rapidly advanced, with a growing workforce, now including women in many new professions, that was trained and ready to continue forward. Most of the rest of the industrialized world was devastated.

To a large degree, the USA was "great" relative to the rest of the world from the mid-1940s to the mid-to-late 1960s because there was very little healthy competition. Most countries were in extended recovery.

Thus the United States was viewed as a place of growth and opportunity, and immigrants from around the world, as they were able, began coming here in larger numbers, as our system was long known for its openness to diverse cultures and opportunities for a happier, safer, more successful life.

Born of a positive view by immigrants and a positive underlying national value of America as a welcoming place, this increase in our immigrant population—from 10 million in 1965 to more than 40 million by 2010—nonetheless had some unintended consequences. Particular among those was the influx of different languages and the slow transition of our systems to accommodate them. Schools, for example, suddenly found themselves dealing with serious language barriers—in some cases seventy-five languages or more spoken in a single school—with limited staffing to address them. The development of those immigrant students and others around them was inevitably impacted.

Meanwhile other trends in American life were unknowingly eroding the environments most needed for critical brain development in young children. The movement from rural to urban and suburban living continued to accelerate. Close-knit extended families were becoming less common.

And in the early 1950s, television became a nationwide sensation, having gone coast to coast for the first time in 1947, at the start of the baby boom.

In many families, especially in those early years, TV was used as a way to share the evening together. But as the fascination and novelty wore off into the 1960s and 1970s, TV time became less a family event than a way to babysit, to keep the kids "entertained" as Mom and Dad did other things. As an unintended consequence of another great technological innovation, more children were on their own more often, with fewer opportunities for family engagement and interaction.

Making matters worse was the commercialization of children's television, as industry insider Chuck Lorre writes:

In the 1980's, Ronald Reagan deregulated children's TV programming. This allowed large toy companies to finance the production of thousands of hours of shows that were designed to sell toys.

Rather than be educated and/or simply entertained, this very vulnerable audience could now be exploited for financial gain. Bad for kids, but good for me. Reagan's mostly unheralded policy shift created an enormous demand for scripts, which allowed me to get my first job in television.

In a matter of months, I went from struggling musician to gainfully employed script-writer. My life dramatically changed for the better, because a Republican president decided the pursuit of profit need not be hindered by the common good.

I've always felt a bit ambivalent about this. For many years I've wondered if my success came at a price. Were children growing up in the 1980's somehow harmed by the cynical, thirty-minute commercials that suddenly engulfed the after-school hours and all of Saturday morning? Well, wonder no longer . . . the damage done to some of those kids was deep and irreparable.[38]

After World War II, our impressive coast-to-coast freeway system was also completed, a further boon to travel and the economy at large, and to those seeking work and opportunity. People could now access jobs in other parts of the country simply by hopping in the car. But one unintended consequence of this remarkable national accomplishment was further disconnection of the nuclear family from the extended one—grandmas and grandpas and aunts and uncles who used to live nearby but now might live thousands of miles away.

The "village" needed to raise a child (we'll discuss this concept in a later chapter, for those of you whose hair is now standing up on the back of your neck) often was unfamiliar terrain, with fewer family members and trusted neighbors accessible to participate in child rearing. Thus another unintended consequence was added to an increasing pile of them: children were spending yet more time on their own or being cared for by strangers rather than relatives. This, of course, further decreased opportunities for family engagement and interaction.

The USA's global advantage dwindled in the 1960s, 1970s, and 1980s as the world recovered from war and competition among countries became fiercer. And because recovering countries still had less-advanced economies, their capital and labor costs were much lower than the USA's, with its robust, high-employment economy. As a result, American companies began looking for ways to tap into other labor markets. This assault on American jobs wasn't so much a matter of United States policy failure, but instead a matter of the rest of the world recovering, with their populations eager to work and willing to do so at lower wages—a great story in itself, but with some obvious downsides to the United States, which had been the predominant world economy.

The invasion of two mid-twentieth-century "bugs" into the USA was the harbinger of things to come: the establishment of the first US Volkswagen Beetle dealership, in 1955, and the Beatles' invasion of American-dominated pop culture in 1964. Global competition in everything from cars to rock and roll was rearing its head after a long rebuild in the rest of the world.

As inflation increased in the USA, jobs changed or disappeared to lower-cost labor markets overseas, unions lost their influence, and wage growth and benefits began slowly deteriorating. Economic issues became a growing concern for more American families, particularly the less educated and therefore less able to transition to higher-level opportunities. In a sense, American capitalism began working against itself, sacrificing American jobs to cheaper overseas labor and technological advances—negatively impacting American families for larger corporate profit and accelerating the disappearance of a robust middle class.

In essence, some of the downsides of capitalism-gone-rogue were beginning to appear. The definition of success in business no longer included the development of a strong middle class and the healthy growth of the majority community. For many businesses, especially large corporations, the definition narrowed to a single focus: increasing value for the stockholder, who was typically wealthy and white, at the expense of everyone else. Greed was "good." A growing gap between rich and poor in America was rearing its ugly head.

Along with other developments changing American family life—more households with both parents working, the growing influence of TV, and the deterioration of the extended family structure as a result of the freeway system—came innovations in food and how Americans ate. This included a proliferation of fast-food restaurants (fostered by the growth of the freeway system and two-working-parent families) and TV dinners and other processed and prepackaged foods with high sugars and salts and preservatives and chemical additives (fostered by less time for meal preparation).

The idea of the family sitting together around the dinner table each evening, listening to and learning from one another, eating fresh food right out of the garden or off the farm, became less and less the American reality. More and more, it was eat and run—and the eating wasn't very healthy. While working parents widely appreciated the convenience of these modern meals, there were again unintended consequences impacting child development. Again, more children were on their own more often, and with far-less-healthy food options in front of them daily, impacting their health, concentration levels, and educational readiness.

Meanwhile, both parents working to "keep up" became the standard for much of America. The use of credit to "keep up" became commonplace, too. Saving became impossible for many, and debt became necessary, acceptable, and easy to obtain. "Keeping up with the Joneses" became a national obsession. Finances became a cause of stress and disruption for more and more families.

These matters were likely not helped any by a popular president in the 1980s who trumpeted a new kind of economics that suggested big deficits were fine and that we could all charge our way to happiness in the here and now—the future would take care of itself. All the demand created by easy credit would in turn create supply; companies would surely hire more workers to fill more jobs. More jobs? Maybe. Higher pay? Not really.

Of course, carrying out that newly formed and untried economic vision resulted in the unintended consequence of higher and higher debt for families. Combined with weaker unions, stagnant pay, deteriorating worker benefits, and rising health care costs, this debt created additional economic stress on households, negatively impacting the positive family environment very young children need for healthy brain development.

The same popular president suggested that much of government was unnecessary—that in fact government was "the problem." In essence, the president of the country suggested that democracy was not working. With the majority of Americans now questioning the need to pay taxes to a system that even the president of the United States was saying didn't function well, our schools, our infrastructure, our space exploration, our care for veterans, and our children, among a long list of other things, began to fall behind the rest of the world's. A majority of America simply decided that they wanted to quit investing in America, and subsequently in our kids' future. Stock market? Hey, great idea! Schools and roads and repairs and maintenance? Not so much.

As two working parents became the norm and one-parent families proliferated, the childcare industry expanded just as rapidly—and, for a time, without much regulation. Some childcare facilities were good places providing excellent developmental care; typically, those were the most expensive options, and not available to most Americans. Many were, shall we say, less than that. Others were simply day-storage facilities that used TV to keep children occupied. Developmental care began to depend more and more on "others." And the families that most needed good developmental care couldn't afford it, so with limited options, they often settled for the "day-storage" care.

Not surprisingly, with Mom and Dad going in different directions more often, and with living standards becoming harder to maintain and money problems becoming commonplace among American families, and with expectations of gender roles rapidly changing and in conflict, divorce rates in the USA also began to rise.

From a post-war low in 1950 to the mid-1980s, the divorce rate ballooned to 50 percent. And while today there is much written about the "myth" of the 50 percent divorce rate—it has steadily declined for more highly educated and compensated families—that number has remained fairly consistent for less-educated and -compensated families for the past thirty years. Of course, the consequence was (and is) more children in high-stress, less-stable environments, particularly children from less-educated and -compensated families, many now with only one parent.

Meanwhile, amazing American innovation has continued its march into the twenty-first century and at a faster and faster pace, again fueled by deficit spending and an economic system paying generous dividends to some of the fortunate better-educated and/or -skilled . . . and to nearly all those at the top. For anyone not in those two groups, however, the pickings get slim.

Technological advances, including smart phones and the proliferation of electronic games for children, boggle the mind. But the unintended consequence has again been fewer entire families at the dinner table engaging with one another rather than with their smart phones and earbuds, texting, tweeting, YouTubing, and Snapchatting. Again, more young children are experiencing less mentorship, less family engagement, and less positive, stimulating interaction with the outside world beyond their phone screens.

The continued push for American businesses to take capitalism to its ultimate redefined goal, efficiency and profit for owners and stockholders, resulted in even greater stress and further changes for many families. These include the often-noted reluctance of workers to use vacation time, the deterioration or even elimination of health care benefits to improve the corporate bottom line, and new technology resulting in layoffs to make companies "more efficient." This "full benefit to stockholders" focus also has resulted in disappearing defined-benefit pensions, declining or stagnant wages, and few accommodations in the form of family leave for the birth of a child. Combined, the result is more family stress over finances, declining family health, decreased family time, worries about the future, and for parents with newborn children, no time to spend with them in the most important developmental months and early years.

The corporate focus on quarterly reports seems to have blinded some business leaders to the fact that, in a sense, they are contributing to their own demise over the long term. Short-term, bottom-line "efficiencies" that increase stock prices and decrease the number of workers (and the pay and benefits that would normally go to them) are creating long-term problems: unemployment, high stress, poor health and nutrition, slowed child development, a growing number of not-ready-for-school kids, and fewer high-functioning adults. With these dysfunctions growing, it has become difficult to find, hire, and maintain a well-educated, trained, and prepared workforce.

For example, maternity leave—a benefit resisted by many companies and corporations—is not just a nice thing to do for families. It's the smart thing to do for corporations. It helps ensure that newborns receive critically important engagement with their parent(s) in the very beginning, and are therefore more likely to succeed in school, and then succeed later in work and life.

In the end, our transition out of World War II and through these many changes meant that most of America no longer resembled the America we thought we were and professed to be on the "family" television shows of the 1950s and 1960s.

Father may have known best, but as we distanced ourselves from the 1940s and 1950s, he often wasn't around to tell anyone, and new roles for Mom (and, over time, for Dad) made consistent engagement more complicated as well.

In fact, in the last half of the twentieth century, our television shows were describing an idealistic "great America" that was rapidly disappearing even as we were watching it in our living rooms.

We loved the sense of nostalgic idealism in those supposedly "contemporary" family shows, understanding somehow what was already vanishing in America while the rest of the world came back to life. We were living that "great America" less and less frequently in real time as the world recovered and became our natural competitors again, and as our own growth resulted in unintended damage to our families, our children's development, and our economic health.

So arose the desire to "make America great again," even though the circumstances that contributed to our global dominance from 1945 to 1965 had long disappeared. Simply put, the rest of the world had rebuilt and caught up and was competing. No amount of wishful thinking or promise making by any single person is going to change that new competitive dynamic, no matter how much some people would like to return to that era.

Meanwhile, all the broad cultural changes noted above (and probably many others unnoted) were also happening incrementally at the family level. As an aggregate, each positive change came with an unintended negative consequence for children—most often decreased family engagement and increased environmental stress. Together, their impact has been huge, and not necessarily positive, on our children's development.

In a sense, while the world was rebuilding and catching up, our own willingness to sacrifice to keep America great, in particular to keep our children at the forefront into the future, was in precipitous decline. While all those other nations were growing stronger economically, we were unknowingly damaging our future with a thousand cuts—mixed, perhaps, with a little too much "what's in it for me."

Near the end of the acclaimed World War II movie *Saving Private Ryan*, a dying Captain Miller (Tom Hanks), having been sent across the battlefields of Europe to find Private Ryan and bring him home, whispers in the private's ear, "Earn this."

The captain, who had lost many men on the perilous quest, was telling Private Ryan to make the same sacrifice for others, and for our country, that he and his men had made.

In the larger context, we are all Private Ryan, saved by those who gave the ultimate in World War II and other wars to protect our country. The captain, as he died, was urging all of us to "earn this." The clear message was that each of us must make the necessary sacrifices to keep our country strong, free, in the lead, and true to our core values.

As the list of unintended consequences might suggest, we are falling short, especially as it relates to our youngest children—particularly those who are living in circumstances we could help improve but aren't.

We are not correcting these problems even when we know how to do it. We are not making the sacrifice. We appear complacent, no longer interested in investing in our country by paying taxes. In the past, we achieved truly great things done for the common good. When's the last time that happened?

Through our complacency and unwillingness to invest in our collective selves, we are harming our country.

Frankly, we should be ashamed.

In his book *The Tipping Point: How Little Things Can Make a Big Difference*, Malcolm Gladwell defines a "tipping point" as the moment of critical mass, the threshold, the boiling point,[39] when a sociological change somehow takes on a life of its own and spreads rapidly across society. Most of Gladwell's examples involve ideas and products and messages that people hope to spread. But he also notes that "behaviors [like ideas and products] spread like viruses," as well.

Have the combined consequences of these many sociological changes created a tipping point for millions of our less-advantaged children?

Have we, ourselves, created the Dark Force that now threatens our place in the world? And if so, can we reverse the consequences, especially for the many children living in the most distressed families?

Has capitalism in the USA morphed into something unanticipated, unintentional, and unsustainable? Have we morphed into a system designed to help the wealthy only—a kind of klepto-capitalism?

Klepto-capitalism is an economic system that replaces democratic government, where the greediest and least inhibited by social conscience are elevated, or elevate themselves, to positions of power in both government and business. It's a system where self-serving policy is developed at the national level and money is accumulated at the very top with little regard for the consequences to society as a whole. In a klepto-capitalist system, huge rewards are given to those often uncommitted to sharing the wealth with those at lower levels who actually did much to produce it.

It appears that we now have a system where a diminishing number of highly wealthy people, many unconcerned with the societal cost, continue to confiscate and hold earnings produced by the majority of others in the system. And it appears that we now have a system where public policy can be bought and sold for the benefit of a few.

The above factors have increased poverty in America many times over. In fact, today's wealth gap is the biggest it's been in our history, including during the Great Depression.[40] And as we now know, poverty is a major source of stress for children, impacting them in negative ways that last a lifetime.

Without realizing the consequences, we seem to have become, as a society, less concerned about the financial, psychological, and physical health of many of our families, and those families, as they struggle to survive day to day, have become less engaged with their own children. This is particularly true of the families in most economic distress. We now have a great many kids in low-parental-engagement, high-stress environments. And when that happens with very young children, their future and ours is at risk.

In short, from the Native American Trail of Tears, to the African American journey through slavery and Jim Crow laws and more sophisticated discriminatory practices, to our more recent failures to value the great contributions of immigrants to America, and now to the deterioration of the middle class, the USA has allowed, even at times encouraged, practices inconsistent with our stated values and laws.

Our unwillingness to make children a top national priority means we've now done the same with our very youngest children—allowed, even at times encouraged, practices inconsistent with our stated values. We have helped create negative environments difficult for these children to escape, yet we appear unwilling to make the sacrifices necessary to correct the problem.

But there is a way; there is light at the end of the tunnel. So, let's move toward the light.

CHAPTER 12

Making Early Childhood Development (ECD) Work in Your Community

STEP ONE: THE CHARGE OF THE LIGHT BRIGADE

I always enjoy visiting my great friend Jerry. We worked successfully together for several years in higher education, building a system dedicated to college student development.

Jerry and his wife, Suzy, now live part-time in Arizona, and as part of their transition, they decided to decorate their new house in a style combining their love of art and movies with their new Southwest location.

The house is near the corner of Roy Rogers Road and Dale (as in Evans) Lane. (Yes, this is true.) Knowing I've collected art and vintage posters through some very fortuitous eBay purchases over a number of years, Jerry called me and asked if I might search the internet for an original poster from the Roy Rogers movie *Song of Arizona*. Lo and behold, on eBay—from a collector in Australia, no less—I found an original 1946 poster from the Australian release of *Song of Arizona*, nearly untouched, with brilliant colors. It now hangs proudly in Jerry's home.

Whenever I walk into his house and see that poster, it takes me back to my early childhood in the 1950s, when television was new and filled with cowboys. The list is long, the names familiar to many of my generation: Hopalong Cassidy, Wild Bill Hickok, the Lone Ranger, Roy Rogers, and many others. What they all cinematically shared was a desire to bring peace and justice and a sense of order to the Wild West. And they were willing to put their own lives on the line to do it.

As thrilling as those heroes and their adventures were, I was often most inspired by the scenes that were not about individual acts of heroism. I was always swept away by those instances when, as imminent danger threatened peaceful men, women, and children and the situation seemed hopeless, those heroes joined forces and arrived just in time to save them.

Or, at the last possible second, a courageous posse of volunteers from town would come together to save the day.

Collective action, when people came together to recover from almost sure demise against overwhelming odds—now that was something!

And that's where we are today.

We are collectively in danger, and our quest must be to dramatically improve outcomes for millions of our youngest children, to keep them from falling into a rapid river and being swept away. Dire circumstances. Overwhelming odds. For many very young children and their families, hopelessness. And for all of us, tremendous social costs.

The central question facing us is, "Will a courageous posse of volunteers come together to save the day?"

Literally millions of our very youngest children are facing bleak futures. Their families are often in economic distress. Their exhausted parents are very wrongly vilified as "takers," for political purposes. In fact, most are working, some two or more jobs, and trying their best to do what's right for their families.

With few resources, they often must rely on low-quality "day-storage care," where children are stockpiled in cribs and planted in chairs in front of television sets.

Given what brain research now tells us, these children might as well be surrounded by silence.

In addition, these children—or their parents, or both—are often suffering from poor nutrition and a lack of good health care. According to the June 2020 census data, nearly 14 million children in the USA suffer from food insecurity and poor nutrition. The parents often don't have reliable transportation, either. In transient, survival mode, they move to different neighborhoods often, in search of lower rent so they can afford to buy gas, make their car payment, get their teeth fixed, and/or buy food.

On top of all that, the parents themselves often had no good role models growing up, so their instinctive ability to prepare their own children for a more successful life is limited.

Whether this is all a result of bad decisions by the kids' parents—sorry, it's rarely that simple—is irrelevant. Placing blame is a waste of time. What matters is that the negative outcomes for many of these kids, slower brain development from both stress and lack of engagement, are impacting us all now and will negatively impact us in the future. A solution will help us all.

Many of the failures suffered by these families are, in fact, the result of generations of our own failure to intercede, no posse of volunteers having arrived to help create environments for success. This is especially true of our negligence since the 1980s when early learning research became clearer. We collectively did little (and in some states, nothing) for our very youngest children in negative environments, despite the available knowledge.

Our first step to recovery . . . to REALLY make America great again . . . is to agree that we must make a fundamental and sustained push to create a nation of well-developed children, beginning at birth.

What we know is that we must get millions more very young children, from birth, into stimulating and formative environments (SAFE), which facilitate synapse-activated neuron engagement (SANE). There they will have a fighting chance to not just survive but thrive, and therefore a better chance to avoid getting caught in the cycle of poverty, which takes them nowhere.

Our collective focus needs to be on improving family environments and therefore children's outcomes, particularly for distressed young children. How do we do that?

Moving to a solution, we must all join the posse of courageous volunteers, or the cavalry. But before charging off to battle, we must reaffirm what we need to take along with us, learning a lesson from the Charge of the Light Brigade. That 1854 action was brave and daring, but few remember that it ended badly because important facts were unclear before the cavalry engaged. They were in some respects the mid-nineteenth-century version of Luke Skywalker, who went off to battle unprepared, at great personal cost.

We need to take on this battle and be the cavalry, but we also need to know what we're getting ourselves into and what it will take to win.

I'd like to think that most of us can relate to how well children learn in great (SAFE and SANE) environments, because many of us have kids and saw their astounding growth in their early years. As my mom used to say, they soak up knowledge like a sponge.

But most of us don't have the experience of advocating for and then putting together collaborative early learning systems in communities—funding them and then making them work on a sustained basis to help children in stressful environments (whether they're rich or poor economically). It will be tougher for us to relate to the "how" of making an ECD system work. The climb up that mountain will be a bit steeper.

So let's start simply.

We must agree on our common goal: to get far more children, especially distressed children in distressed families, into stable environments where they can experience positive stimulation and more rapid brain development.

There are many peripheral things that must happen to achieve that goal on a broad scale, but none of them should take precedence over focusing aggressively on getting more and more children into SAFE and SANE settings. And nothing should take precedence over keeping them in those settings so that they can thrive and be ready to start school, then mature into contributing, successful adults.

If a collaborative effort toward that end does not involve tracking and increasing the number of children being moved into SAFE and SANE settings to improve their school readiness, then that collaborative effort has lost its way, or has not yet found its footing, or simply hasn't found the money required. Sadly, a lack of consistent funding (in other words, no funders making the issue a true long-term priority) is the norm. We will discuss that shortcoming in a later chapter.

A community-based early learning system that's firing on all cylinders will consistently measurably increase the number of children in SAFE and SANE settings and report the indicators and outcomes that give confidence progress is being made.

We know a strong community-based ECD system can be developed. It is being done in a few communities by connecting nonprofit-based professional "family stability specialists" (or "support specialists" or "navigators" or "facilitators," or whatever title is chosen locally) to families with very young children. The facilitators then use best practices to educate the parents or other caregivers on better parenting skills. They also connect families to the human services they need most to improve stability and lower stressors, economic and otherwise, in the household.

A second part of Step One is simply this:

We must work together to focus on doing whatever else it takes—such as increasing the opportunities in our communities for unique learning experiences; improving/increasing needed social services, including health care and nutrition; or advocating for support from state and local governments—to stabilize more families and decrease stress in the home.

When we work together with a common focus, we all become the calvary, helping create more and more SAFE and SANE settings in each of our communities. When we do this on a large enough scale, we'll have a fighting chance to improve the future of all children, ultimately improving the future for you and me, for our communities, and for the country as a whole.

Our how-to sections, next up, will focus mostly on the community level, where direct work with families and children will occur. But we will also discuss ways to move forward on a national scale. Along the way, it will become clear what you as an individual can do to help.

CHAPTER 13

Making ECD Work: Preparing for Action

STEP TWO: *MISE EN PLACE*: INGREDIENTS FOR SUCCESS

I didn't learn to cook until I was past fifty years old. My wife, Alvarita, is a great cook, so admittedly I took advantage. That ended when our kids permanently left the nest, and she announced that either we'd be eating out a lot or I'd need to learn to cook.

I couldn't even boil water at the time.

However, I'd recently read that if you want to keep your mind sharp, you should challenge yourself to learn new things. And having just added cable TV to our home, I was fascinated by the proliferation of interesting cooking shows, which made cooking look as much like an art as a "you have to do it this way" science project. I decided to accept Alvarita's challenge.

One of the first lessons taught in cooking school is the French culinary concept of *mise en place*. All really good cooks follow it as a central tenet. It means having everything in its place before you start cooking—preparing and organizing the proper ingredients. I didn't attend a formal cooking school, but I did attend several cooking classes taught by respected local chefs, and every one of them mentioned the importance of mise en place if you want whatever it is you're cooking to turn out successfully.

In that vein, if we're going to cook up a successful ECD design—a recipe for success—let's explore the detailed ingredients that we must have in place to implement the broader strategies discussed in the previous chapter.

Mixing metaphors, let's start out with a curveball and talk about ingredients we typically lack these days: patience, focus, and sustained commitment.

As a country, we are well known for our lack of patience and, lately, for our lack of sustained commitment. And mission drift, or lack of focus, is quite common; it results in all those meetings we go to where everyone talks in circles for an hour and then agrees to do it again next week.

Both patience and sustained commitment served us well in World War II, and again shortly after that in the space race, when we put a man on the moon. Those two events had very clear goals, and focus was not much of a problem. But somewhere along the line—perhaps after our "sustained commitment" to the Vietnam War—sustained commitment (at a difference-making level) has not been our calling card unless someone was making a whole lot of money as a result of that sustained commitment.

Our War on Poverty might be one example of where we have had sustained rhetoric over time, but not a sustained, consistent effort, with programs funded and defunded, started and stalled. And of course this inconsistency is important in the context of early childhood development, because poverty is a leading indicator of where to find the children who will benefit most from ECD efforts.

Poverty in America seems to be an unstoppable river that sweeps people downstream with it, and we appear to live in a society that rather intentionally keeps the floodgates open and the current swift, thinking everyone should sink or swim, even if a pretty large number of people started with lead boots.

It is hardly arguable that our inconsistent, fifty-five-year War on Poverty has only partially succeeded, while the status quo has largely remained in place . . . or, more accurately, those with status seem to be getting more and more of the quo.

> Like the misdirected blame on schools for poor student performance (a great many young children are simply not ready when they get there), perhaps our emphasis in ending poverty should be redirected, as well.

Might we be more successful if we make sure our youngest children don't fall into the river in the first place, as Archbishop Desmond Tutu famously suggested? We can do this by placing far more emphasis on helping those distressed families with very young children. We should make increasing resources and developmental assistance to those specific families an urgent national and community priority.

We will address our approach to poverty in more depth in chapter twenty-five. In the meantime, let's identify our mise en place list of essential ingredients for the ECD effort. The first ingredient is all too easy to find:

- **Families in distress (often economic), with very young children (ages newborn to three)**

All communities have distressed families with very young children. Many of those families live under financial or other stress that endangers their children's early brain development. Others live in very low-engagement environments. Often both things are true. Families and children in dire circumstances deserve specific attention, because the children most in danger also represent our greatest hope for remarkable outcomes. We need to know where they are and what they need in order to decrease their stress and increase positive engagement.

- **Knowledgeable, passionate, articulate leadership at the local and national levels**

   This is a vital ingredient to any successful venture. These are typically focused, well-informed people who take up the early learning cause, successfully engage others, help organize all the other ingredients needed for a successful outcome, and keep everyone focused on the collective goal: children in SAFE and SANE settings where they can more fully and rapidly develop.

These leaders must also be able to communicate the basic elements of brain development research and/or bring in others who can do so.

- **Key nonprofit organizations already working with families**

This work will require these organizations to come together in new, far more intentionally collaborative ways that are responsive to existing local conditions and relationships. Most will be asked to review what they are already doing for families with young children and to double down on that effort, placing a higher priority on using their resources there. For example, a food bank that operates on a first come, first served basis might agree to designate specific times for families with children under four to be served as a first priority. Or a county might set up a partnership between its senior centers and local childcare centers, so seniors can read to the young children on a scheduled basis.

The list of possible participants in such a community collaboration, and the potential important benefits derived from their participation, follows a bit later in chapter fourteen. Many of these nonprofit organizations are small but powerful assets in the communities they serve, as we saw so vividly in the tremendous contributions they made during the coronavirus pandemic.

- **Commitment from the larger community**

   People in the community need to step forward. The professional community-based "worker bees" who already partner with families and often staff local nonprofit organizations, or our preschool, kindergarten, and first-grade teachers, cannot carry this load alone if the effort is to be successful and sustained.

All communities must intentionally become positive, stimulating "villages" for our very young children.

- **Commitment from business leaders**

  Often missing from ECD efforts such as this are business leaders, influencers who can help move the needle far more rapidly through their participation. If their active participation is not included in the mix, the final product will suffer greatly for it.

- **A constant commitment to quality standards**

  This becomes key as the collaboration forms and community commitment grows. Because of resource constraints, it's not always possible to reach the very highest standard of quality, but it *is* always possible to know what the standards are, to set the bar high, to know how close we are to reaching it, and to know what we need to reach it.

As we'll discuss later, measuring and reporting is powerful, even if the news is sometimes bad.

And what must be measured is not only the quality and success of service to the families and children (indicators of child and family development), but also the standards that apply to well-functioning coalitions working toward collective impact (indicators of successful collaborative efforts).

Later we'll highlight helpful research that can guide community coalitions working to establish an early learning community committed to the highest standards of service and administration.

- **Funding**

  Perhaps the most difficult thing to find as you peruse the farmers' market of fresh and available ingredients in your area will be a different kind of green: money. Without it, no national ECD effort, and few community efforts, will thrive. Short-term (one-, two-, or three-year) funding is frankly insufficient, not to mention illogical, in an effort that requires sustained work over decades. But not having money up front should not be a deal breaker, as the realistic hope of funding can spur action.

Chapter twenty-one will propose what might be considered some wild and crazy funding ideas, including a chance to "meet the Beatles."

- **Effective advocacy**

  Growing new, passionate, and effective champions and donors is as important as finding money in the first place. The process of growing money and donors revolves around effective advocacy spurred by consistent and helpful information, another vital ingredient to a successful early learning coalition. Much of effective advocacy centers on proper preparation and timely presentation. "Be prepared" is not a phrase exclusive to the Boy Scouts, as chapters twenty-one and twenty-three will reveal.

- **Boldness**

  Here's another vital ingredient: boldness. Ask big and expect big commitments to something critically important to everyone in your community. Be passionate. Be loud. Create momentum.

The next chapters will discuss each of these vital ingredients in more detail. Among them, hidden between the lines, is something we discussed in the opening of this chapter: persistence and perseverance. For while it may not be rocket science, it does take time to start up any venture and expand it to scale. When that venture involves true brain science and changing our priorities and how we do business in collaboration with others, it may— no, it will—take significant time.

CHAPTER 14

Making ECD Work: Going Big by Keeping It Small

AVOIDING BULKY BUREAUCRACY: SPEEDING IMPLEMENTATION

Warren Buffett, chairman and CEO of Berkshire Hathaway and one of the world's most successful investors, once wrote that he's skeptical "about the ability of big entities of any type to function well."

Said Buffett, "Size seems to make many organizations slow-thinking, resistant to change and smug."[41]

Berkshire's corporate headquarters still has only a handful of employees, with almost all the managing work left to its unit managers. "It is a real pleasure to work with managers who enjoy coming to work each morning and, once there, instinctively and unerringly think like owners,"[42] Buffett said.

In other words, he lets his trusted workers who are nearest the issues run the business, consistent with its broader guidelines and strategies.

In our communities, those trusted people nearest the issues "who enjoy coming to work each morning" to help families that need it are primarily the locally based nonprofit service providers.

These small, efficient organizations are annually vetted by numerous others (funders of all sorts) to ensure their outcomes are being achieved at reasonable cost. In many cases they are reviewed by trained community volunteers associated with the local United Way; by staff and volunteers from community foundations and private family foundations that may fund the nonprofit; by city, county, and state agencies that provide funding; and maybe even by corporate funders.

Fraud, abuse, and poor outcomes are rare among these efficient nonprofits, because they tend to be small by corporate standards and locally funded and administered. The great COVID-19 crisis showed their strength under enormously trying circumstances. They proved time and again that they know their communities and know how to deliver. There are occasional bad apples, of course, but they are rare.

All of which is to suggest that the way to get the best, quickest results for the lowest cost in creating an ECD system is to focus locally. Depend on local organizations that are thoroughly vetted, and let them get to work using fundamental, research-based guidelines. And budget from the ground up: meet their needs in full first, and then provide funding up the chain as necessary.

We can develop a community-based national ECD effort by keeping it small and local—letting the local experts work together around the fundamentals outlined in this book. These fundamentals are grounded in research and direct experience. There is common agreement on most of the fundamentals, and relatively common acceptance in practice.

We don't need a huge federal or state bureaucracy to put the design into practice, community by community, on a nationwide basis. In fact, having one would likely be a wasteful mistake. Should there be some structure? Yes. Should that structure be huge? No.

At the same time, we have to *go big*. We have 15 to 16 million children in poverty, and millions more on the edge of poverty and in families experiencing high stress. About 7 million of these children are three years old or younger. If a family stability specialist can work with thirty families, that means we need about 235,000 family stability specialists to reach our families and children in distress. At an average salary of $50,000 per worker (including benefits such as health care, sick leave, and vacation time), that adds up to something big: roughly $12 billion. Per year. And that's just the on-the-ground staffing.

Now would be a good time to recall that we are currently paying well over $500 billion a year in social costs for those who have not been successful in navigating our current system. And that $12 billion for early childhood development will go a long way over time in reducing those huge social costs.

Even while keeping implementation local, we can go big by getting that money to communities across the nation that are already deeply engaged in family-support activities, with existing administrative structures and existing community support. We don't need lots of new money for administrative expenses. Some new money? Yes. Incremental? Yes. A new bureaucracy? No. In essence, we keep it small, using battle-tested and -proven nonprofits, existing research on early learning methodologies, and existing research and learning on community coalition building. Add to that existing overview and evaluation processes. It's *all* there.

Yes, if funds come from federal or state sources, some staffing will be necessary to pass money through, to establish general guidelines consistent with research, and to review indicators and outcomes with funding partners in local areas (such as United Way or community foundations). However, if the proper broad strategies, based in research and experience, are well articulated in providing simple and administratively inexpensive pass-through funding to well-respected, community-based oversight agencies, the need for further checkers checking other checkers and another big bureaucracy and more administrative overhead is greatly reduced. Well, OK . . . unnecessary.

The infrastructure to oversee finances and outcomes already exists in most areas, either regionally in rural areas or locally in medium-to-large metropolitan areas. Highly professional and well-respected United Ways and community foundations are excellent examples.

Given our ability to go big by keeping it small (local), now would be a good time to take that trip to Mayberry and shake off that discomfort with the phrase "It takes a village to raise a child."

CHAPTER 15

Making ECD Work: The Power of the Village

STEP THREE: UNDERSTANDING MAYBERRY R.F.D.

Everybody I know used to hate group projects in school.

Almost always, somebody in the group would not come through. Having the right people in the group was hard, because the members were often selected by someone else. And even if they weren't, there always seemed to be a really poor reason someone didn't come through.

So how does that relate to the beloved TV show featuring the town of Mayberry?

The actual name was The Andy Griffith Show, and later Mayberry R.F.D. One online source describes it this way:

"Andy Taylor is the widower sheriff of the small, sleepy North Carolina town of Mayberry. Andy and son Opie live with Aunt Bee, who takes care of the family. Andy's deputy is his bumbling but neurotically hilarious cousin, Barney Fife."

In this small town, everyone knows everyone, and they are constantly seen taking care of each other, especially little Opie. Anyone who has ever watched *The Andy Griffith Show* and seen everyone in Mayberry hover over Opie knows exactly what the phrase "It takes a village" is intended to mean, in a very positive sense. Everyone in Mayberry has an eye out for Opie, often to his great consternation.

Everyone in Mayberry engages with Opie. They all watch over him, protect him, encourage him, and provide him with various forms of positive stimulation. *That's* how strong brains develop and how kids get great. We collectively need to be that way for all our kids if we really want to make America great again and again through time.

While we can make our own individual contributions to such an effort, the scale of our current problem is so large, and the assistance needed so important, that we must become far more effective in reaching the millions of children who need improved care.

Yes, the parents are the kids' first, best, and most important teachers, no question about it. And that should not change. But in some cases there is only one parent, or none at all. Vitally important are aunts, uncles, grandparents, brothers, sisters, good friends, childcare givers, teachers, preachers, and even sometimes the mail carrier or the barber or the neighbors or the grocer at the checkout stand.

Those wonderfully quirky folks of Mayberry have been on TV for fifty-five straight years now. That should mean that many millions of adults have seen, and therefore have some understanding of the positive meaning of, "It takes a village to raise a child." The concept is not something to fear or that should inspire negative comments.

My group projects, at least in school, never seemed to work out as well as things did in Mayberry, where everyone was on task with Opie. But we are all older now, with experience and lessons learned. If we set our minds to it, we can do much better in this important ECD group project. In fact, we know these efforts can work (without forming huge government programs) because there are some good examples in a few communities already.

Boston, Massachusetts; Charlotte, North Carolina; Nashville, Tennessee; New York, New York; and San Antonio, Texas, are currently operating "gold standard" pre-K programs, according to a study commissioned by the de Beaumont Foundation and Kaiser Permanente.[43]

This ECD stuff is one group project we have to make sure works well in *every* community, with high standards, sustained funding beyond just a few years, and implementation on a large scale.

If we don't have lots of the right participants doing their jobs—helping develop millions of kids in communities throughout the nation, turning them into community and national assets—the effort to "make America great and keep us there" will be an even tougher climb than it already is.

We know that building an effective community-based early learning system will be a bit complex. To summarize, here are the factors we will need to consider:

- **SAFE and SANE settings**

  We've already talked about the importance of creating SAFE and SANE settings, in which early development is enhanced. A SAFE environment is free of the adverse childhood experiences that create stress and slow brain growth by inducing negative chemicals in the brain. Once achieved, a SAFE setting is where one can engage in various positive, stimulating activities, which turn on electrical synapses that connect billions of neurons in the brain. Synapse-activated neuron engagement (SANE) enhances developmental learning by hardwiring important pathways in the brain, giving children a fighting chance for a better start and a better lifelong journey.

- **Parents and caregivers as critical partners**

  We've revealed how surprisingly young children can start learning complex things like music, math, scientific principles, reading, languages, and social skills like working cooperatively. But that's only IF (and that's a big IF) they are surrounded by caring mentors in a stimulating environment, with the parent often being the first, best, and most important teacher.

- **The vital need to start very early (birth through age three) for best long-term benefits**

  We've talked about the intensive and extensive interventions that are necessary (and typically not available) if we wait too long to give our most distressed kids SAFE and SANE settings . . . and we've been doing little to nothing for millions of our most distressed children.

- **The tremendous financial cost of delay (to all of us)**

  We've also talked about how most late-stage interventions are far more costly—and again, typically not available—and often far less effective than preventive measures. We've discussed how we can't miss the opportunity to be proactive when the negative consequences of inaction are staring us in the face.

- **The national ripple effect of "not ready" children**

  We've discussed the fact that there are huge numbers of young kids entering school *today* who aren't ready to learn and succeed. And we know that lack of readiness in these children creates longer-term negative consequences for our schools, other students in our schools, our teachers, our businesses, our economic competitiveness, our social costs, our community health and safety, and the children themselves, who are left behind from the very beginning and then struggle as adults.

- **Parents whose circumstances make them less likely to rear successful children**

We've acknowledged the difficult circumstances of many parents and distressed families, especially those in poverty. Some of the parents have been impacted themselves by delayed development. Many are experiencing financial difficulty, a lack of reliable transportation, unsafe home environments, and other stressors that inhibit family stability. Many are in poor health, poorly nourished, and highly transient, constantly moving to more affordable housing in less-safe environments. Their ability to afford good childcare is limited, and their ability to travel to larger, in-place early childhood sites is limited and sporadic.

• **A strategic shift of focus to end the cycle of poverty**

We've been frank about how poverty is systemic in our society, and that if we continue to focus first on "ending poverty" rather than focusing on the children in poverty, we may never make the headway necessary to improve outcomes for children on a grand and consistent scale. Over half a century of a largely inconsistent War on Poverty should prove that. Increasing resources to families and children most likely to "fall in upstream," in order to keep them out of the raging river altogether, therefore makes all kinds of common sense. Successful children who grow into successful adults can help end poverty one child at a time. That's a more reachable goal in a more reasonable time frame than the fifty-five-year War on Poverty, which still hasn't reached its goal.

While past efforts to address poverty have focused on jobs for the parents or other parent-focused economic strategies (which often place them marginally above the poverty line and reverse when the economy falters), the suggestion here is that we first focus on improving the stability of families with very young children: lower household stress, facilitate more engagement between parents and children, and encourage more positive engagement by secondary caregivers, as well. In short, we want to make young children the focus of the War on Poverty, by preparing them for later success no matter the circumstances. If those children succeed later in life because we've all helped their brains develop very early in SAFE and SANE settings, we are more likely to break the cycle of poverty nationally, because so many of those children will do so individually.

This is a longer-term view than our current "get the parents a job" focus, but it's far more likely to be *permanently* successful in the long run. Don't let the children fall into poverty upstream.

- **Stopping the blame game**

Finally, we've talked about the fact that it doesn't matter whose "fault" it is that the parents and kids are failing. The negative impacts affect us all—in our neighborhoods, in our schools, in our businesses, in our social costs and taxes, and in our ability to compete in an ever-more-competitive world. What *does* matter is that together we can improve this situation, and cut our costs, by focusing on a solution: creating more and more SAFE and SANE settings for children.

We've already identified Step One to developing an ECD system in our communities:

We must agree to maintain a laser-like focus on creating more and more SAFE and SANE settings for more and more children in our communities, beginning with families in most distress, where our gains will be largest.

The next step is equally simple to articulate: our communities must all become Mayberry, "villages" working in intentional, research-based collaborations to help all our children be ready for school and therefore likely to succeed later in school and life.

This means we must form communities across our country that collectively have the development of very young children as a priority. We must become loud and aggressive and effective early learning communities.

As I've noted earlier, most successful early learning communities to date have used family stability specialists (or the equivalent) from nonprofits already working with families in distress. These specialists connect families with services to create household stability and lower economic distress, while also working with them on positive parenting skills.

Our communities have a lot of existing assets in common that we can put to use on behalf of very young children and families. And distressed children and families have a lot of things in common to which we must effectively and consistently respond over an extended time. We'll lay those commonalities on the table in the next chapter and explore how to use them to give every child the best chance to be a successful and contributing adult.

Think of each community effort as a unique jigsaw puzzle: the goal is to bring together all the pieces needed to create a wonderful picture. Each puzzle will have different pieces and a somewhat different picture based on specific environmental factors, geography, and local resources and issues.

Each community, large and small, must carry the spirit of Mayberry, with multiple resources focused on helping our children grow into successful adults.

CHAPTER 16

Making ECD Work: Answers in Your Own Hometown

"Here he comes to save the day!
Mighty Mouse is on his way."[44]

STEP FOUR: MIGHTY MOUSE IS ALIVE AND WELL!

We visited our older son, Ethan, and his young family in Orlando recently, and they were excited to take us to the Universal Studios version of Harry Potter's world. It was full of hidden passageways, magic windows that only worked with certain kinds of magic wands, and other hidden features known only to those who were informed and paying attention. In fact, I walked right by a wall that led to the entry to the entire village of Hogsmeade, home to even more enchanting wizardry, and I didn't even know it. I missed the secret pathway and I was standing right there.

My eleven-year-old grandson and nine-year-old granddaughter didn't miss it, however; they were much more informed and aware than I was.

And thinking about it, that's kind of how the world—the real world—works, too.

Paying attention and being informed—knowing the important details and taking informed action by making the right moves in the right place—is critical to finding one's way to success.

And when it comes to early childhood development and early learning, success involves putting together a jigsaw puzzle of important pieces that are likely already out there, often right next to you, including some small-but-powerful Mighty Mouse heroes ready to help save the day. For readers far younger than me, Mighty Mouse was an early TV cartoon character, a small mouse in a superhero suit and cape, who always "saved the day." A modern equivalent exists in our local nonprofits. There may be no superhero suits involved, but they're small, knowledgeable, and efficient organizations, and they regularly save the day for many people in our communities.

And that brings us to one secret path to successful community-based early childhood development—using existing community resources and the community coalition approach.

Some coalitions may need to be county-wide or regional, with several organizations in nearby smaller cities taking part.

Here's where you might find Mighty Mouse heroes for your community effort; some or all of these may be critical pieces of your community's jigsaw puzzle to unleash the "power of Mayberry" in your community.

- pre-K, kindergarten, and first-grade teachers
- school district superintendents
- childcare providers and associations
- Head Start, Early Head Start, and state-funded preschool leaders
- early childhood developmental screening programs
- Community Action Agencies
- Communities in Schools organizations
- housing authorities
- homeless shelters
- Boys & Girls Club or equivalent
- YMCA/YWCA
- domestic abuse shelters
- health departments
- Nurse-Family Partnerships
- hospital birth-center leaders
- United Way
- community foundation leaders
- corporate foundation leaders
- private family foundation leaders
- nonprofits providing housing assistance, nutrition assistance, childhood screenings, health assistance, job training, etc.
- nonprofits serving specific minority populations, such as Native Americans, African Americans, Hispanic populations, Eastern Europeans, Asian populations, and so forth
- Boy Scouts, Girl Scouts, and similar organizations
- college or community college experts in social services, childcare, or early learning
- library systems (literacy focus)
- children's museums (play-to-learn focus)
- corporate leaders as personal champions (especially those with children)
- Rotary Club leaders

- Chamber of Commerce leaders
- economic development organizations
- educational service district leaders
- public television leaders
- churches, church volunteers, and church leaders
- city council members and leaders
- state and local political leaders, especially early learning advocates
- senators and congressional representatives
- newspaper publishers, editorial boards, and writers
- television news leaders

Count how many of these people or organizations are already in your community or region—I'll bet there are several. What if they all had a common goal of helping develop the most progressive early learning community in the United States? What if many of them agreed to participate in a collaboration to measurably increase the number of children in SAFE and SANE settings in your community? This goal is vital to having young children ready for more by four, ready to thrive by five, and be great by eight.

The community coalition approach means using key resources already operating in most communities (often a number of relatively small nonprofit agencies focused on family stability, complemented by churches, elementary schools, libraries, museums, etc.). These nonprofits, through innovation and by adjusting their priorities, can advance early learning comprehensively and affordably through intentional, focused collaboration. It's not simple, but it can be and has been done. The larger challenge is growing the effort to reach the vital tipping point (effectively reaching a majority of those in need) and then sustaining it over time.

All the fundamental pieces required to make a wonderful picture of family supports and enhanced developmental opportunities for young children already exist in most of our communities. They just aren't arranged, coordinated, and pieced together around a common goal of early childhood development, with a focus on creating more and more SAFE and SANE settings, with more and more children measurably entering into those environments as a central measure of progress. Neither are they sustainably funded at a large enough scale, but we'll get to that piece later.

While every community puzzle will have generally similar pieces, each community will create its own picture of customized resources, players, and issues to address. There will be unique spaces to be filled by these various organizations in order to stabilize families, lower stress, and increase positive engagement between caregivers and young children.

Fortunately, there are a number of communities that are already awake on this issue; they have identified and implemented various early-adapter approaches (models) to bring early learning to the young children and families who need it most.

The most successful outcomes to date have been achieved by communities that built and sustained family resource centers in the areas of most need, with specialists (or counselors or navigators) working with children and their parents and other caregivers continuously for five years or longer.

Together these communities have built more SAFE and SANE family settings in which their children can thrive. But these efforts, often called Educare centers, are very expensive to build ($8 million to $12 million each) and then sustain (about $2.5 million a year). And they have limited geographic reach. Families in distress, remember, don't have reliable transportation, so a site-based effort, as good as it may be, is often limited by that factor as well as by the high initial cost.

Only twenty to twenty-five Educare centers currently exist in the United States, in a similar number of communities, and efforts to build them have been ongoing for nearly twenty years, funded by some very large, capable, and well-endowed foundations. While these centers are great additions to the ECD effort, and they've proven to be effective, they probably won't be the solution to the early learning puzzle in most American communities. They are simply too expensive. They are not widely replicable or independently sustainable. And instead of twenty of them, we probably need twenty thousand. Given the cost and replication barriers, it seems more sensible to attempt to replicate Educare-quality training and indicator/outcome evaluation in home-based settings, using family support specialists from existing nonprofits.

Given that Educare models appear most effective but are expensive and therefore not widely replicable, perhaps our Early Head Start programs, for children ages zero to three, would offer the easiest and fastest expansion opportunity. They already exist, they use research to make continuous improvements, and they have past support in Congress. But they are also burdened by loads of bureaucratic paperwork and carry historical baggage from past years that keeps them from being fully utilized in some communities. This is one area where the "build back better" concept should be incorporated, no matter who's the president of the USA.

Another option is to pick an existing family support or early learning program in the community and bring it to full scale.

With that model, a single local program (typically one administered by a human services nonprofit) is selected based on its strong track record of helping families in distress, its work with other providers of important stability services, and its support from key leaders who can influence funding.

As with Educare, this model works for the families it reaches, but accessibility is often limited by funding. In this case the funding is needed to expand to such a huge scale that many other vital early learning components in a geographically diverse community might be given less attention and funding, or perhaps be eliminated from consideration altogether. Borrowing from lots of smaller Peters to pay a really big Paul is a somewhat risky way to go.

While it's true that tough choices have to be made because resources are limited, *not* taking advantage of what already exists in many regions—a loosely organized group of efficient nonprofit organizations working with distressed families—seems like an interesting choice to make.

Often these diverse organizations enable geographic diversity, ethnic/cultural diversity, funding diversity, and a set of extensive, community-based supportive relationships, a combination of qualities you probably won't find in any single organization. Which brings us to the novel idea of uniting many existing organizations into "community cooperatives"—strong, committed local collaborations specifically focused on helping distressed families with young children through early childhood development.

While each individual organization in the cooperative may have a narrower focus, such as housing, food, health care, or transportation, most already work with distressed families and cooperate at some level with other assisting organizations.

In this proposed design, the central questions for each organization become "How can our organization, in concert with others, focus more on assisting distressed families with very young children? How can we work in partnership with parents and others to stabilize those families? And, how can we play a role to create more and more SAFE and SANE family settings for more and more children?" Each collaborating organization retains its initial focus or mission (housing, food, health, etc.), but agrees to bring more thought and resources to the issue of early readiness of the youngest children, ages zero through age three. Sustained assistance in the transition to school (thrive by five) and then to children reaching third-grade reading proficiency on time (great by eight) would be even more powerful. Research affirms that success in these early stages can help bring the cycle of poverty to an end as these children age into successful adults.

In this collaborative model, it becomes vital for the proposed coalition to identify the strengths and weaknesses of the present loosely organized system of local services as they relate to the most vulnerable children in the service area.

The group has the capability to identify needed changes or priorities to strengthen and better link the loose system into a more dynamic, focused coalition with an overarching goal. For example, the collaboration may assess that the first priority for assisting distressed families in the community is hiring far more family stability specialists, and the second priority is strengthening the local food bank system.

Working through this strengthened coalition, individual agencies would agree to advocate for those common priorities necessary for it to become even stronger. In this case, for example, all coalition agencies would advocate for more family support specialists (even if those specialists will be assigned to other partner organizations) and more resources for the food bank (even though they, themselves, are not the food bank).

In this scenario, if a particular organization's priorities are also those of the coalition, it doesn't have one "self-serving" voice (its own), but instead the voice of an entire community of organizations advocating for that needed community resource. And over time, as the needs of one organization become the needs of the coalition, each in turn receives the advocacy help of the others.

This can be a pathway to a more robust early learning effort in almost any community.

The major strength of the community cooperative concept lies in the fact that almost all communities of size—those with a population of, say, thirty thousand or more—already support a number of the organizations needed. In smaller communities, these organizations likely exist on a county or regional basis.

Existing community-based organizations already have administrative structures, funding sources, and a host of supportive community members; most also already have trained and competent staff working with distressed families. They can easily be brought up to speed, if needed, on the latest effective curriculum in working with families; they have proven positive outcomes; and many are already working in loose partnership with one another.

In many communities, they are also geographically and ethnically diverse as a group, serving many neighborhoods, and collectively they already have working relationships with many of the families and children and other caregivers most in need of SAFE and SANE settings.

What they *don't* have working independently is the depth and breadth of assistance that distressed families with very young children typically need to stabilize and move forward. But collectively they *do* have depth and breadth. As collaborating organizations, for instance, they might have experience and training in nutritional food, safe housing, accessible health care, job training, parenting training, early learning concepts and training, childcare improvement and training, childhood developmental screenings, and mental health. They might have measurement and research capability, advocacy and marketing expertise, staff to work with targeted families, and so on. There may be particular weaknesses in the depth and breadth, but it becomes the coalition's job to identify those and advocate to improve them in whatever way is necessary for the better health of distressed families with young children and the better health of the community.

Tacoma, Washington, used momentum to aggressively expand an early learning effort, Prevention Partnership for Children, that began around the year 2000. It evolved into an effort to ensure third-grade reading proficiency, then to assist kids in the vital transition from middle school to high school, and then from high school to the next level.

Originally these were independent efforts—loosely collaborating, if at all.

The local United Way sponsored a presentation by researchers and outside professionals on how to achieve "collective impact." The energy and excitement generated helped to form what's now being called a "community gemstone," using the tools identified combined with the efforts of strong local nonprofits and committed leadership.

That "community gemstone" is now Graduate Tacoma, an intentional, focused collaboration of organizations working with community partners on educational issues from early school readiness to high school graduation.

In the early 2000s, Tacoma's high school graduation rate hovered in the 55 to 60 percent range. Now it's 89 percent. And given the research, one can expect that many of those successes will multiply into larger gains as those graduates move into their twenties.

Most communities *don't* have a formal early learning coalition with a formal set of goals to provide a constantly growing number of SAFE and SANE settings, or a formal agreement to cooperate and communicate and measure and report around that set of common goals. They also *don't* have a small but single-minded independent administrative structure to keep the coalition focused, moving forward, and communicating.

What they also *don't* have is funding to provide them with the staff and time to collaborate with others; and they *don't* have funding to evaluate the outcomes of the cooperative goal, or to follow progress on agreed-upon indicators of success, both for the coalition and for the children and families with whom and for whom they are working.

For a passionate, focused coalition, these are the things they must develop to bring creative, cooperative, effective work alive—to inspire and motivate them as they work together on a common goal, finding solutions to facilitate healthy brain development in very young children, in concert with their families.

Hang on, because if you and others put this machinery to work, you might get to eighty-eight miles per hour pretty quickly. Great Scott!

CHAPTER 17

Corporate Leadership, Early Childhood Development, and Long-Term Thinking

STEP FIVE: "THE THREE LITTLE PIGS" AND OTHER BEDTIME STORIES

My generation had its own kind of early learning program. It usually consisted of graham crackers, a small bottle of milk with a thin cardboard pull tab on the top, and a sleeping mat. That was followed shortly thereafter by seeing Spot run with Dick and Jane, or similar stories. These were read to me or with me by my parents, my grandparents, my aunts and uncles, and my kindergarten teachers, my next-door neighbor, and my babysitter, to name a few. You know, the whole village.

My favorite story was always "The Three Little Pigs," although I have to say "The Tortoise and the Hare" was a close second. But the "The Three Little Pigs," now there was a story that kept you in suspense, wondering how those pigs were going to keep the wolves at bay while the dumber, lazier pigs wasted their time building these flimsy structures meant only for immediate shelter. I mean, here I was, only four or five years old, and even I knew those houses weren't going to cut it when the wolves came huffing and puffing. Thank God at least a third of the pigs knew a little something about long-term thinking and building things that would stand and last.

And that, of course, brings us to the corner of Corporate Social Responsibility Road and Smart Investment Lane in our trek through Early Learning Town, or as we sometimes call it, Mayberry R.F.D.

In the 2016 presidential primary season, Bernie Sanders talked a lot about what corporations should do, like giving working parents maternity leave and having a family values agenda. But it seemed to me that Bernie's problem in communicating about this issue with the business side of America was that he never made it clear why corporations should be doing this for their own good, other than saying something like "Every other major country is doing it," and "Family values matter," and "Last place is no place for America."

Bernie was correct, of course. But being correct didn't help corporate America see why such an agenda could be in their own self-interest, and that's where Bernie fell short.

What generally convinces people to do or change something is that they see that the idea directly benefits them, or at least is not harmful to them. And in this particular case, the direct benefits of family-friendly policies to businesses are very clear, even if they aren't commonly articulated or enacted.

Supporting maternity leave is about supporting the healthy development of children in their very earliest years, so that their little brains are stimulated and their neurons are activated, so they will be ready to succeed in school, then in jobs, then in life.

It's simple. Paid family leave makes sense for every business that wants to build something for the long term: a "steadier and readier" stream of good workers for the life of the company. It's one of the biggest complaints of businesses today, their inability to find "good workers," yet the majority of those businesses have short-sighted policies that contribute a great deal to the very problem they lament.

The same can be said of health benefits and living wages. These things create stable environments for families, cut down on adverse childhood experiences, and help prepare children to succeed in school, become good workers, and lead happy, successful lives.

Certainly, these benefits help families. And providing such benefits does put some immediate financial pressure on the company. But much like the third little pig taking the time to build a brick house while the wolves are on the way, smart corporate leaders who think long term will understand that these aren't just costly, "give me stuff" ideas that will benefit other people. Instead, they are smart ideas that will benefit the company by stabilizing families, creating stronger schools and communities, and providing exceptional workers over time.

Smart corporate leaders, the long-term thinkers, will take the leap and do it; they will decide to build the house of brick. It's called good, smart, visionary leadership. On an institutional scale, such behavior is identified as corporate social responsibility. These companies take action that helps others, and while it may not make their bottom line look pretty next quarter, it makes their companies' and communities' long-term future look far brighter.

But just like the three little pigs, not all of whom saw the imminent danger, maybe only one corporate leader in three will see the light and do the right thing—the more difficult, long-term task that will benefit their company later by benefiting their workers and their community now. And this visionary, strategic approach is why "great corporate leadership" is actually quite rare. It risks upsetting the corporate quarterly-report applecart, because building with bricks instead of straw costs a little more up front.

The majority of corporate leaders face constant pressure to do what's best for the immediate bottom line, to do what's best for the stockholders, who want their quarterly dividend to look better. So most of those corporate leaders will end up getting stuck in the briar patch—but I think that's a different bedtime story. It probably wouldn't be fair, and it's too easy to call them impatient and greedy little pigs.

"The Pied Piper" is a different story, too, but I think there are some lessons for corporate leaders that apply there, as well.

In this case, we should be searching for the good pied pipers, not fretting about the bad ones. We need visionary corporate leaders, often those with children themselves, to get everyone else to hop on the early learning bandwagon in our communities. These are the leaders who will see the long-term benefits of early childhood development: the ready kids, the better schools, the higher graduation rates, the better workers, the more successful and healthy families, the breaking of the poverty cycle, the lower social costs, and the upper hand it will give us in a worldwide economy. If asked to do so, a number of them will play the music, sing the song, and help lead the community to a better place. They can be key influencers of other important community leaders.

It's important that nonprofit leaders not make the same mistake as the two little pigs who got blown away. If you want your coalition to be solid as a brick house, then strategically involving key corporate leaders better not just be on your "agenda." It must be part of your active, ongoing behavior.

You need to know which corporate leaders in your community will pick up the flute (or was it a piccolo?) and lead the parade. And you need to be aggressive and successful in enlisting them to join you. Otherwise, you risk having a house of straw, too.

CHAPTER 18

Making ECD Work: Being the "Best"
Early Learning Community

STEP SIX: COMPETING WITH A STANDARD OF QUALITY

In the beginning of my own work helping form a community coalition around early learning, I made a number of **speeches** to various groups and to potential nonprofit partners in which I suggested that our community become "the best early learning community in the United States."

Curiously, my speech was met with very different responses depending on whether I was talking to nonprofits helping families . . . or just about anyone else.

Business leaders responded positively, perhaps being more naturally competitive. Teachers responded hopefully, knowing what a tremendous difference such an effort could make in their own work. Citizens, who worked in a variety of businesses, tended to respond with enthusiasm to the idea.

But nonprofits—my cohorts who commonly worked in collaboration with many others just to be effective and survive fiscally—responded less favorably, much to my surprise. To them, wanting to be "the best" sounded like a desire to compete with other communities or even with other nonprofits within our own community. It sounded exclusive, like a zero-sum game, where if "we" achieved fame for being the best (and the fortune that might come with it in terms of grants or other fiscal support), it would be at the expense of others. And they cared about all families and they cared about their partner nonprofits, not just the families in their own geographical area or their own nonprofit.

I was stunned by the resistance to being the "best" from those in my own community, in my own area of expertise. Yet in retrospect, I understand how I could have been clearer in my messaging.

In my thoughts, we would be competing against a standard of excellence, always wanting to meet those high standards. Being the best didn't need to be exclusive of others. In fact, I hoped that every other community could join us at the highest level of service to families and that we could help them if they asked for our assistance. I assumed that most of the other nonprofits in our community, who were already working in some way with distressed families, would find a positive connection, and make a positive contribution, to our effort to be "best" relative to quality standards.

In the end, this unexpected experience turned into a great example of how both words and assumptions have tremendous power, and how understanding (not just messaging) is the key to good communication.

The competitive advantage of a community with high-functioning schools, high graduation rates, outstanding workers, low crime rates, falling poverty rates, and shrinking welfare
rolls is tremendous. But as my surprising experience demonstrated, even obviously positive
outcomes don't translate into automatic participation by others. Misunderstandings can
easily slow the effort. So it's important to be clear about the coalition's goals, on multiple
levels.

The community coalition's general **strategic (big-picture) aim**, as we have discussed,
would be to work more closely together to improve very young children's overall care, with
a focus on improving their early brain development by creating SAFE and SANE family
settings, and expanding the reach of the coalition to constantly add more children and
families.

Each community coalition might define their aim somewhat differently due to differences in community circumstances; cultural sensitivities; geographic issues (urban, suburban, rural, distance, and accessibility); and the various organizations involved. However, the
overall strategy needs to be clear, concise, powerful, and reinforced regularly, and it must
help guide everyday work.

The more **tactical (action-oriented) aims of the coalition** would be the following:

- To help primary (most often a parent or parents) and secondary caregivers
  lower stress in the family environment.
- To help primary and secondary caregivers understand and implement positive, stimulating engagement activities with young children in their care, often
  through one-on-one work with family stability specialists, family support
  specialists, or similar professionals familiar to coalition members.
- To analyze the developmental stage of the young children involved, and to
  suggest appropriate ways to enhance development.
- To connect families and children to the resources they need in order to stabilize the families, lower their stress, and increase positive parental engagement.
- To aggressively advocate, as a group and as individual organizations, to
  increase the agreed-upon priority resource(s) required for success in working
  with distressed families.
- To work within the coalition to identify ways each organization might contribute to the work of others to improve outcomes for all.
- To consistently measure and report (to the community, funders, political and
  business leaders, and all working partners) the indicators and outcomes (good
  news as well as areas for improvement) for the children, families, and coalition
  efforts. *In particular, reporting the growing number of SAFE and SANE family*

settings and the growing number of young children in them should be a primary focus. So should measuring and reporting the developmental progress of the children in those settings.

- To follow up with the families (and the schools) as children move into state- or federally supported early learning systems such as Head Start, or into school systems, to ensure successful transition.

The above steps should be followed by further aggressive advocacy (marketing, communication, persuasion) to educate key leaders and potential champions about existing early learning research and the positive outcomes being achieved.

As an end result (outcome), we are talking about improving the brain development and readiness of many more very young children, whether they are in the care of their parents, friends, or neighbors; more highly trained childcare professionals; or state or federal ECD programs staffed by well-trained personnel.

Wherever the care is being provided, we want to improve the level of care, make the care more developmentally appropriate and effective, and/or expand the reach of high-standard care that already serves a population of children.

By "developmentally appropriate" care, we mean care that does these basic things (tactical action steps taken by the family support specialist working with the family):

- involves the parents as much as possible and helps them be successful in positive parenting
- reduces stress and improves stability in the child's environment, particularly in the household but also in secondary caregiver environments
- facilitates positive, consistent engagement of all caregivers with the child
- engages the child in age- and developmentally appropriate learning, with a sensitivity to unique cultural issues
- focuses on the child's social, emotional, and cognitive development
- includes parental goal setting and consistent tracking, often with third-party assistance
- improves developmental knowledge and training of all caregivers
- connects the parents and family to other needed services to stabilize them and lower factors leading to adverse childhood experiences and stress, which may delay development
- involves follow-up on goals and timely family support to improve stability

- tracks and reports statistics regarding children's developmental and educational transitions (including school readiness and achieving third-grade reading proficiency) consistently among coalition members
- continues to aggressively expand its reach to serve more parents and children

Larger community coalitions may include tracking and assisting children and families through middle school into high school, and then from high school to college or work.

In reality, all three models articulated in chapter 16, with the rapid expansion of Early Head Start being a fourth, are likely to eventually evolve into community coalitions of sorts. Educare centers reach out to many other organizations in their geographic areas of focus; programs chosen to be the central early childhood administrative source in their community do so, as well. Both often act as de facto leaders within the larger working groups they form over time.

In either the community coalition model or the "choose an existing program" model, expansion to reach more children and families will happen slowly as funding grows through various means, often depending on the passionate advocacy and strength of vision of the coalition itself.

One way to prioritize service, given limited resources, is to target neighborhoods near kindergartens and elementary schools with high rates of free and reduced lunches. There is a strong correlation between high rates of free and reduced lunches and high rates of poverty and everything that goes with it: less parental engagement, more stress in the home, and low rates of readiness for school.

Where resources to promote early childhood development and family stability are initially limited (which is almost everywhere in our nation), targeting neighborhoods with kindergartens with free and reduced lunch rates of 60 percent or higher will likely reach children most in need as a first priority.

As measurable progress is made and as more resources become available based on that proven progress and successful advocacy, the goal would be to reach schools/neighborhoods with free and reduced lunch rates of 50 percent, then 40 percent, and so on. This is the type of strategy that the coalition itself, working together, needs to develop based on elements in their own community. There might be better ways to target a particular community depending on local circumstances; it's the job of the local coalition to work on the best solutions.

CHAPTER 19

Making ECD Work: Measuring Standards of Excellence and School Readiness

PROVING PROGRESS

I was a pretty good baseball player. I played third base primarily, but at one time or another growing up I played every position on the field, including pitcher and catcher. Knowing more now about how the brain develops and how learning occurs, I realize that playing all those positions helped me understand the game better—shall we say, from a "multiple neuron, multiple synapse" point of view. I see the game of baseball as a ballet, with movement all over the stage by every player on every pitch.

Until the year I grew six inches and could barely walk and talk at the same time without falling over, I was usually one of the better players on my team. But in my awkward teen years, I lost my speed. During those years in summer ball, I knew I would be in a battle to make the starting nine, because we were a championship team with good players—county champions two out of the three years I played. I knew I had to be ready to win an infield position.

I remember preparing myself by going into our basement and throwing a tennis ball against the wall as hard as I could, reacting to the bounce, preparing my defensive instincts. I'd move closer and closer to the wall, continuing to throw hard and at different angles, trying to improve my reaction time and my ability to catch hot shots with quick and receptive hands. Other times I'd force my younger brothers to throw me grounders, or to catch my throws from farther and farther away as I tried to improve my arm strength and my accuracy. In the end, I could throw a ball consistently and accurately on a hard line from third to first base.

In any event, each summer when the season started, I was more prepared than my peers defensively because I knew something about what it meant to be ready. But in all my years of playing ball, I never had a coach who showed me how to hit.

When I was young, hitting had come easy, but as I grew more awkward as a teen, none of those natural instincts seemed to work anymore. So, to get on base, I developed a discriminating eye at the plate; I walked a lot, often leading my team in walks. Then I proceeded to clog up the bases because I couldn't run very well.

My senior year in high school, my baseball career came to an end. I was an all-star when I was young, and a gold-glove fielder as a teen, but my lack of mentoring in hitting finally caught up with me. I was doomed to a short "career" as a singles hitter with a great eye and get-on-base ability, but no speed. I was destined to fail at higher levels where they could throw more strikes. I had no hitting fundamentals to carry me. I wasn't ready.

By now you can probably surmise where this is going in our early learning discussion. We are sending a lot of young singles hitters out there, young children destined to fail at higher levels because they weren't engaged and coached by positive mentors early in their development. They aren't ready.

And of course they rarely know they aren't ready until they keep striking out and then give up.

They have no way of knowing what "readiness" means, because in most cases they haven't lived in SAFE and SANE settings that foster good brain development, which would have helped them quickly learn what it takes to be more successful, to hit metaphorical home runs.

Fortunately for those of us tasked with helping young children be ready, science is telling us now how we can measure our children's readiness. It's our job to take this knowledge and make it happen. Measure it, then improve it for each child we can reach.

A 2016 study about children's development notes "that from infancy to school entry, children follow a fairly typical continuum of social and emotional skills acquisition," including the following:

Infant

- is aware of separation from adult caregiver
- learns to be soothed by others and to self-soothe
- participates in early social interaction such as eye contact and smiling
- responds to their name
- exchanges vocalizations/sounds
- expresses a variety of emotions such as delight, sadness, fear, and anxiety

Toddler (1 to 2)

- recognizes and interacts with a number of people
- focuses attention and plays more independently
- expresses a greater range of emotions, verbally and nonverbally
- recognizes the changing emotional state of others
- acts more assertively in social interactions

Preschool (3 to 4)

- develops emotional connections beyond immediate family
- understands the difference between socially acceptable and unacceptable behavior
- persists with challenging tasks without becoming unduly frustrated
- pays attention for increasingly long amounts of time
- avoids interrupting others
- displays delay of gratification skills around taking turns and sharing toys
- identifies and articulates their own and other people's feelings
- increasingly manages their own strong emotions in socially appropriate ways
- solves some social problems independently

And there we have it: ready for more by four.

Why are these milestones important?

Well, quoting from the same article, "a recent study found that children who, in kindergarten, are better at resolving conflicts with peers, understand emotion, and are helpful and cooperative with others are more likely to become well-adjusted adults who have jobs and contribute positively to society."[45]

Obviously, if they arrive at pre-K, kindergarten, or first grade with these skills, then the children's parents and other caregivers, the entire "village," had to have been involved in stimulating those big little brains in positive ways between the ages of zero through three. If the children haven't met those milestones, it's important to know that, so you can remediate.

There has also been a lot of work in the field of early social and emotional development. As a result, there are now many verified ways to measure skills such as social competence, emotional competence, behavioral competence, and self-regulation. In fact, there appear to be as many as 120 different measures solicited from the nineteen ECD researchers who contributed data to the above journal article. Not all of them were equal in quality and ease of use, of course. The authors identified six strong candidates for widespread use.

In addition, there are multiple ways identified to measure cognitive readiness in very young children. Measurable skills include mentally processing new information, relating it to already-learned information, and communicating about it.

As with social and emotional development, there are a number of commonly agreed-upon benchmarks and indicators of development along the continuum from infancy to toddler to preschool and beyond. For children, benchmarks include the following:

- speaking clearly in short sentences
- counting to ten or higher
- understanding fact and fiction, truth and stories
- following brief directions in two or three steps
- talking about or explaining an event in proper sequence

Many of these measures have been developed by researchers in coordination with professionals in the field working with children and their families.

Similar milestones and assessments are available to measure physical readiness and executive function (planning, organizing, assessing, staying on track, etc.).

Given this wonderful array of great work in the field of early childhood readiness, and our ability to measure it reasonably well, why are so many of our children not ready when entering school? A *New York Times* op-ed from June 2016 addresses the question head-on:

> One of the paradoxes of American politics is that [early childhood development] is an issue backed by overwhelming evidence, enjoying bipartisan support, yet Washington is stalled on it.
>
> Gallop [polling] finds that Americans by more than two to one favor universal pre-K, and Clinton and Sanders are both strong advocates; Trump has made approving comments as well . . . So, in this presidential campaign, let's move beyond the debates about free tuition and minimum wages to push something that might matter even more: early childhood programs for needy kids . . . America's education wars resemble World War I, with each side entrenched and exhausted but no one making much progress. So, let's transcend the stalemate and focus on investing in America's neediest kids.[46]

While we wait for that investment to happen in Congress (big yawn?), our major national foundations and corporations and communities should move ahead on this issue anyway. While doing that, we have to be aware that measuring the readiness of the young children we reach must not be the only goal. Great by eight (third-grade reading proficiency on time) is vital, of course. But making sure our community coalitions remain strong, pointed in the right direction, and moving toward excellence is a trick in itself; we must also regularly measure the coalition's progress ("How well are we working together?") and report back to the group.

Over my many years of work in collaborative ECD efforts, the biggest stumbling block tended to be losing collective focus, drifting away from the coalition's central mission. In this case, the mission should be pretty clear: something like "making sure every child from age zero through three in our community lives in a SAFE and SANE setting and makes the transitions to reach school ready to succeed."

Mission drift appears to be a common systemic shortcoming among coalitions, probably due to the fact that each participant, almost by definition, has a slightly different mission and agenda than the others. The natural tendency is to drift back toward everyday "my mission" activities, leaving coalition building (adjusting one's own work to facilitate the work of others) behind.

And when money is a factor—which it inevitably is, since early childhood development is so poorly and erratically funded—action among coalition members tends to shift to the low-hanging fruit, activities that can be accomplished right now with available resources. Often these activities are not unreasonable, but they only marginally move the coalition toward a standard of excellence in fostering behaviors that make a significant, sustainable developmental difference for the children and families. For example, the coalition might focus on affordable housing as a weakness in their area, and then that effort takes over the focus of the coalition to the degree that the effort to get more distressed children into SAFE and SANE settings loses its momentum. As this important but secondary issue becomes a more comfortable and accepted focus for the group, efforts to expand the reach to more distressed children and families, and to provide other types of quality assistance that lower stress and eliminate adverse conditions, get lost in the shuffle. It becomes a case where doing good is not doing good enough.

Remaining focused on the ultimate mission—more kids making measurable progress in more SAFE and SANE environments—is paramount.

In the context of an ECD system, the vision and activities always must facilitate moving young children, especially those in distress, along a measured and reported continuum toward more rapid brain development, school readiness, and third-grade reading proficiency—the indicators of potential long-term success. Closely connected to that effort is working with the families to improve parenting and engagement skills and to reduce household stress.

What other "standards of excellence" should a birth-through-three collective-impact coalition strive to meet? To answer that question, we must return to the research on early childhood brain development, as well as to the specific circumstances of the coalition members and their community. In general, however, the following questions would be central to gauging the coalition's progress in advancing the brain development of children ages three and younger:

1. How many children and families are we collectively reaching?
2. Of those families, how many have children age three or younger?
3. How good are we, individually and collectively, at helping those families facilitate SAFE and SANE settings? How do we measure that success?
4. Are we consistently using research-based practices to lower stress and other risk factors in these households?
5. What specifically research-based practices are we individually or collectively using? Have they been successful?
6. What vital services are most needed to do this?
7. Do we need help from others in the coalition to be more successful, individually and collectively, in creating those SAFE and SANE settings? If so, what kind of help do we need?
8. What are we doing to expand our reach to help *more* families with very young children, particularly those in distressed environments where brain development in children is most at risk, and where our work will likely have the greatest impact? How many children/families are in need, and what are our annual goals for expanding our reach, in terms of numbers?
9. Can we expand our reach by changing how we work with others in the community or within our coalition?
10. Have we agreed on a shared way to internally measure and report our progress (for instance, an online spreadsheet stored in the cloud that only coalition members can access, outlining issues and services provided to each family, to avoid duplication by others)?
11. Do we have a plan to build leadership in the community, particularly among business leaders who can influence others to bring money to the effort?
12. Have we identified coalition members' common needs that will be critical to their collective success, and are we working together to advocate for those common needs?
13. Have we identified all coalition members' concerns about their ability or willingness to continue working together on this effort?
14. How many children ages zero to three have we measured for readiness, and what is our success rate?
15. Are we successfully transitioning three-year-old children to preschool or pre-K programs to continue their development? How are we measuring and reporting this with consistency?

Seriously, if we aren't helping create SAFE and SANE settings within families with very young children, and if we aren't lowering risk factors and increasing positive engagement in those families, and if we aren't increasing our reach to more and more families, and if we aren't measuring and reporting the developmental progress of those children regularly and consistently, and if we aren't successfully helping transition those kids to preschool and pre-K programs, then haven't we lost our way? Readiness now creates the strong likelihood of success in adult life. Great by Eight is not just a marketing phrase or a book title—it is a critical goal. To reach third-grade reading proficiency on time first requires our children to be ready for more by four, and then to thrive by five (be ready for school).

One example might be my home state, Washington, an early leader in ECD efforts. For all our efforts, the National Chamber of Commerce Foundation recently rated Washington forty-sixth out of all fifty states for overall enrollment in early learning programs and poverty-based participation.[47] Perhaps the standards of excellence set by the collective impact coalition aren't high enough. I'm not sure that's accurate, but it's a question worth asking. If we aren't successfully reaching more families, what's the point of all that peripheral work?

Of course, other coalition work is important.

Collaboration is important.

Building relationships and trust among community organizations is important.

Dreaming is important.

Working for social justice and equal treatment is important.

Collecting data to better understand relevant issues is important.

Sharing learning is important.

Advocacy is important.

But if all the activities of the coalition do *not* result in more young children in SAFE and SANE households, either its standards of excellence aren't high enough, or its advocacy efforts to expand vital service need more emphasis.

CHAPTER 20

Making ECD Work: The Importance of Laser-Like Focus

STEP SEVEN: THE KEYS TO SUCCESSFUL COLLECTIVE COMMUNITY IMPACT

As I write this, it's opening day of the baseball season, early in the spring. Thirty major league teams have spent the last month preparing to play ball. They've been regaling their fans with updates on new players, new organizational approaches to compete and win at the major league level, and new developmental approaches for the minor league teams to "ensure success over the long term."

About seven months from now, only one of those thirty teams will have won the World Series, meaning twenty-nine will have "failed." This scenario happens every single year.

Which proves things don't always go as planned.

If you've ever worked for a company or served in any capacity with an organization, you probably understand exactly what I'm talking about.

Making early childhood development work well through a community coalition includes lots of planning, lots of hard preparation, and a hefty amount of failure.

The tipping point—critical mass, the point at which a community brings ECD to scale— still seems a long way away, unfortunately both at the local and national level.

In communities that have seen the research and fully understand its importance and the consequences of doing nothing, there's lots of planning and discussion about alternatives and approach. And, frankly, there has been substantial action and investment to make it work, mostly focused on four- and five-year-olds. This is often because there are already structures in place—such as pre-K, Head Start (or state-funded versions), and/or universal kindergarten—that can be more easily leveraged into the effort.

The same can be said of the more sophisticated charitable foundations. They are aware of the ECD gap and have made various attempts to address it.

Yet none of those plans have been focused on children three and younger. And none have resulted in making early childhood development effective at a large enough scale, for a long enough time, to reach critical mass—that is, to reach well over half the young children living in high-stress, low-engagement settings.

No effort has seemed sustainable, much less able to expand its reach to the thousands in any community of size that need the help. This vital work is often characterized by the following progression: start, stop, fall back, start, marginalize to other hot priorities, lurch forward, fall back. And very few of those efforts have aggressively targeted children at the critical age range of birth to three, with the exception of Educare, which is the least-replicable design due to its ongoing expense.

Of course, we must recognize and appreciate what's been done to make programs like Head Start and pre-K more accessible, particularly to four- and five-year-olds. The federal government and some states continue to fund those vital programs (even if at reduced or status quo levels), and many foundations continue to support them, and insist on seeing improvements in their performance indicators and outcomes, even if they typically fund them for three years at the most (and may not fund direct service, such as family support specialists to work with caregivers).

And many communities have made huge strides with literacy programs as well as "play to learn" programs, particularly through the growth of better-designed, research-based children's museums.

Yet millions of four- and five-year-olds who need Head Start and similar developmental boosts remain unserved. And the vast majority of children in the vital zero-through-three age range live in states that are early learning wastelands—states completely devoid of intentionally designed, community-based programs that work with families to nurture very young brains.

There are various methods used to determine the "best" states for early education, resulting in different lists of which state is best or worst. Six states, however, spend no state funds on prekindergarten: Idaho, Montana, North Dakota, South Dakota, Wyoming, and New Hampshire. Twelve other states with state-funded pre-K have no three-year-old children enrolled at all.[48]

It's time for our country, and especially our most poverty-stricken states, to stop falling back and start being far more attentive to children ages zero to three. Yes, things may go wrong no matter the planning. Nevertheless, we must make the leap in our communities now or continue to suffer the long-term consequences later—to our worldwide competitiveness, to our schools, to our pocketbooks, and, most important, to our children.

MAKING COMMUNITY COLLABORATIONS WORK

How can we take our loosely coordinated local agencies and make them work more effectively together to create measurably positive outcomes? Happily, there are good answers to that question, wrapped in outstanding research about how collaborative efforts work best.

A company called FSG is involved in research and consulting around what they call "collective impact." Defined as "broad cross-sector coordination" in a "highly structured collaborative effort" around a shared agenda relevant to all participants, the collective impact approach has expanded into many communities.

In FSG's insightful articles "Collective Impact"[49] and "Channeling Change: Making Collective Impact Work,"[50] published in the *Stanford Social Innovation Review,* they identify key components to succeeding with this approach, based on significant field research and their own consulting efforts. They suggest that learning to work together through the collective impact model is imperative to "achieving large-scale progress against urgent and complex problems."

Having worked in several community-wide collaborations prior to the release of FSG's initial research in 2011, and having struggled through many of the phases the company identifies in a collective impact effort, I can say that their framework rings true, and I would recommend it for careful consideration. A good starting place would be their article "Early Wins in Early Childhood: A Case Study,"[51] which can be accessed online for free.

While not wanting to rewrite all of what they have already labored to write so well themselves, FSG's Five Conditions of Collective Impact are important to share here. These key conditions, as they note, "distinguish collective impact from other types of collaboration":

- **A common agenda:** All participants have a shared vision for change, including a common understanding of the problem and a joint approach to solving it through agreed-upon actions.
- **Shared measurement:** Collecting data and measuring results consistently across all participants ensures efforts remain aligned and participants hold each other accountable.
- **Mutually reinforcing activities:** Participant activities must be differentiated while still being coordinated through a mutually reinforcing plan of action.
- **Continuous communication:** Consistent and open communication is needed across the many players to build trust, assure mutual objectives, and create common motivation.
- **Backbone support:** Creating and managing collective impact requires a separate organization with staff and a specific set of skills to serve as the

backbone for the entire initiative and coordinate participating organizations and agencies.[52]

FSG also notes that it is "important to recognize that the initiative must build on any existing collaborative efforts already underway to address the issue." In most communities, as I have previously identified, there are likely numerous nonprofit human service organizations already doing some form of work to support families and children, serving as a platform from which to engage.

The job of the coalition is likely to encompass these or similar goals:

1. Develop a widely shared understanding among the partners of the community's "loose" system currently supporting families, particularly those with children ages zero to three. The families' needs and the available resources are likely to differ widely between communities; this is the fundamental reason why a community-based system with local knowledge is so important.
2. Develop widely shared agreement on the number of families with young children currently being assisted, and the number of families that urgently need assistance but aren't receiving it, and their general location (perhaps using free-and-reduced-lunch or assisted-housing data).
3. Develop widely shared agreement on the types of services most needed in that specific community to stabilize families and lower their stress, in order to help create SAFE settings to enhance brain development and early childhood development.
4. Develop an assessment tool to determine where along a continuum (weak to strong) the adults are in understanding how to work toward a SAFE and SANE setting for their children.
5. Develop a widely shared and consistently used assessment tool to reasonably measure (notice the phrase is not "precisely" measure) the developmental progress of children being assisted.
6. Develop a widely shared, consistently communicated advocacy message regarding the coalition's top priorities that will allow it to improve the quality and quantity of services to families and children. These priorities may change as the coalition matures and additional resources are brought to bear.

Every community probably already has a number of nonprofits or other entities with professionals who go by a title like family support specialist, family advocate, or family service navigator. In each of these organizations, the job of what I will call the family stability specialist often entails the following responsibilities:

1. Assess the family environment (economic and social stressors, level of engagement with children, history of stability, etc.).
2. Assess the child's current developmental level, or arrange for that assessment.
3. Assess the adults' understanding of the importance of a healthy environment and of active, positive engagement with their child.
4. Develop a family progress plan, including services needed to stabilize the household environment and lower stress, and what might be called a parenting-skills component—a plan for the family and child to work together to enhance positive engagement. As the needs of each family will differ, customized plans are often developed.
5. Act as a navigator, advocate, and support for the family to help it advance along the plan—connecting family members to other organizations and assistance in the collaborative effort.
6. Measure and report success back to the host organization of the family support specialist, which then enters the data into the coalition's measurement system.

It is not uncommon for these specialists to work with as many as forty families, which frankly is an overload given the stress factors impacting the family, the likelihood of imminent instability, the lack of immediately available resources to facilitate stability, the time required to assess the family, and transportation time (particularly in more rural areas). But given the already-difficult issue of funding and sustainability, that workload will likely have to suffice.

The most critical measure of success of any collective impact coalition focused on ECD will be a growing number of families and children being assisted by family support specialists (by whatever title); the number of environments being improved; and the number of children reaching developmental indicators.

FSG also suggests that these preconditions must exist for collective impact to have a fighting chance: *an influential champion, adequate financial resources, and urgency for change.*[53]

I'm hoping this book can serve as a wake-up call, to create urgency for change that anyone should be able to see. But finding dynamic, influential, passionate local leadership and adequate financial resources is where the wicket gets a little sticky in my experience, as well as in FSG's.

Regarding leadership, FSG states, "We have consistently seen the importance of dynamic leadership in catalyzing and sustaining collective impact efforts. It requires a very special type of leader, however, one who is passionately focused on solving a problem but willing to let the participants figure out the answers for themselves, rather than promoting his or her particular agenda."[54]

I would restate this point somewhat differently, because it could be taken to mean that the leader should refrain from demanding constant attention to certain agreed-upon commitments, goals, or needs.

In fact, demanding constant attention to agreed-upon goals is vital to the focus and eventual success of a collaborative effort. Avoiding mission drift and circular, never-ending conversations requires frank, sometimes uncomfortable discussions, most likely initiated by the visionary leader.

Sometimes letting participants figure out the answers for themselves requires strong reaffirmation of what everyone agreed on in the first place, and typically a focused and passionate leader will be the first to remind everyone. This reminder might be mistakenly labeled as an unwillingness to let the participants figure out the answer for themselves, when instead it's simply an effort to keep everyone from talking in circles about things already agreed upon. In these discussions, strategic direction is often confused with the tactics to get there. Tactics are debatable, while strategic direction has already been decided—or should have been.

Nor should a visionary leader hold back in giving an opinion. Speaking up means the leader is part of the participant group, confidently offering opinions and making a case as others might, but also ensuring that everyone is heard and all ideas are considered. When the group is deciding on tactics, the visionary leader must be open to any carefully considered decision to go in a different direction on a specific issue, and must align behind that collective decision and carry it into the community. But the visionary leader will always continue to demand focus on agreed-upon vital goals and administrative expectations, and require solid reasons for rehashing strategic direction.

And then we come to money. Here is where my experience in providing, and later funding, direct service takes a somewhat different path from that outlined by FSG. As noted, FSG suggests that funding is a *precondition* to forming a collective impact collaboration, partly because the group needs a separate "backbone organization" to coordinate and administer it. To some degree, there is truth in that statement; money is woefully lacking in human services. Attempting to "find" funds while you're trying to convince organizations of all types to join an urgent but unfunded effort, no matter how popular, is difficult.

On the other hand, many human service practitioners would argue that money often follows success, rather than paying for it up front.

In other words, coalition progress and indicators of success will help drive funders' decisions.

Successful collaboration requires vision and passion and a "don't take no for an answer" mentality. In some cases, those very strengths can jump-start a successful collaborative effort based on an inspiring vision and the willingness of coalition members to make initial sacrifices.

In this case, sacrifice is most likely to include their time and potentially some of their fiscal resources. By "raising awareness of the importance of the active coalition efforts through passionate advocacy," coalition members increase chances for outside funding.

Having money as a precondition is often a nonstarter, at least in the human services arena. *In the case of early childhood development, nothing should serve as a nonstarter.* Passion and sacrifice and the ability to envision how a plan *might* receive funding support "if we plan and advocate well" may need to come first.

The hope that coalition partners have the power to convince funders to move in their direction is often enough, in the short term, to bring the collaboration together.

But as FSG notes, there will need to be a backbone structure to organize many of the group's coordinating functions, and to ensure constant and consistent communication within the group.

In the early stages, this may require dedicated staffing by one or more of the participating organizations, or perhaps short-term pooled funding for staff, until more permanent funding is garnered. This is a critical piece of collective impact start-ups, based on my experience with them. But not having everything, including funding, figured out and in place at the very beginning should not stop efforts to make it all happen.

Creating a staff backbone might be a way for coalition members to prove to themselves early they can achieve small victories by working together in new ways.

Finally, money is a constant issue, and the main reason for the "start, grow, fall back, restart, stumble, stop, restart" pattern that is a constant among nonprofit efforts, and in early learning start-ups in particular. Early learning has long-term outcomes. Many funders, it appears, can't see that far or wait that long. That's a big roadblock, and a bigger mistake.

Collective impact studies sometimes imply that the efficiencies found through newly aligned coalition efforts will lead to far more reach at marginal cost. And that may be the case when it comes to quality of service and ease of access to some services; these might improve greatly as coalition members find ways to work in more aligned fashion.

Unfortunately, without increased funding, it would be exceedingly rare for direct-contact staff to expand their outreach to more families. In most cases, each staff member is already working with upwards of thirty, sometimes forty, families to help create more stable home environments. Put simply, while collective impact collaboration could facilitate more direct work with families, it is not the magic answer for scaling efforts to critical mass.

Without question, more money for more staffing, sustained over a longer time, will be necessary.

And more money for supporting services—either through a change in funding emphasis or the addition of new funding—must become available in order to reach critical mass.

In the early learning arena, it will be very difficult to make substantial headway unless major funders join forces to think about how to fund such an effort differently. More aggressive funding and a much longer view are essential to reaching critical mass. Starting up a community coalition takes time, building trust in a collective impact model takes time, learning and adjusting based on unique community needs takes time, staffing up and training takes time, achieving interim performance indicators and outcomes takes time, and scaling efforts to critical mass takes time. Without aggressive, sustained funding over many years, achieving all these goals will be impossible. Frankly, to date, it *has* been impossible.

While other things can derail a collective impact effort, and we'll cover those shortly, sustainable funding is where we will go next. Let's go meet the Beatles, who (you will be surprised to learn) can help us with one of the most vital elements of fund development.

CHAPTER 21

Making ECD Work: Secrets to Sustainable Funding

STEP EIGHT: MEET THE BEATLES

If we learned nothing else from the presidential primary season and subsequent election in 2016, it was the power of celebrity—how far it can carry someone in this day and age, and how many others are willing to jump on board in association with it.

People flocked to be near Donald Trump. Heck, they flock to be near Kim Kardashian. People flock to watch reality shows that are nowhere near reality. It's all about star power.

I first became acutely aware of the impact of star power when I was a college senior. I was fortunate enough to have been elected vice president of the student body at Eastern Washington State College. I was in charge of all student-funded activities, and part of my responsibility was to bring in popular bands for concerts.

I decided to book a group called Kenny Rogers and the First Edition. They had their first hit song out, "Just Dropped In (To See What Condition My Condition Is In)," and they were about to release their first album, with another song that would move up the charts, "Ruby, Don't Take Your Love to Town." They were emerging stars, a rock group with country roots. Several year later, in 1983, Kenny Rogers (now without the First Edition) and Dolly Parton would team up on a massive hit, "Islands in the Stream," and tour together in concerts that cost the promoters a rumored $750,000.

At the time, Eastern Washington State College was small, with only about thirty-five hundred students, many from rural areas of the state. Many others commuted from Spokane, about twenty miles away. About a thousand students lived in the dorms on campus. Concerts were held in an old multipurpose building that could hold about three thousand people. It was rarely full, however, no matter the draw. Partly that's because our budget was limited, which restricted whom we could afford to book. The talent was typically not the biggest names in entertainment.

But with Kenny Rogers and the First Edition, we got lucky. Their song was shooting up the charts, and their rock-country-folk appeal fit our demographic, so the group was very popular. Because it was their first hit, they were still affordable. And they were between stops at larger venues, so they could do our college gig on their way to bigger shows, cutting costs further. We got Kenny Rogers and the First Edition for something like $1,750. Remember, this was before his collaboration with Dolly Parton.

The house at Eastern was going to be packed to the rafters, a truly unusual event. Eastern Washington students, as well as a number of outside visitors from Spokane, were going to see a group everyone wanted to see, and we got to be "almost first."

And then disaster nearly hit.

Ninety minutes before showtime, with the venue already beginning to fill up and an excited buzz in the air, the group still had not arrived. At the venue, I was getting nervous. Then I received a call from San Francisco. The airport there had been fogged in, and Kenny Rogers and the First Edition were just getting ready to board the plane for the nearly two-hour flight to Spokane. They asked if they should reschedule. My honest answer was no, because no dates were open on the short calendar remaining in our year. Also, ticket refunds would have been a disaster; our rather unsophisticated operation didn't provide concertgoers with ticket stubs.

The group's road manager then asked, "But will they wait for us?" And this simple question, filled with no small amount of angst, prompted my introduction (and maybe theirs) to the true power of celebrity.

"Are you kidding me?" I responded. "I've never seen such excitement for a performance on our campus. But if you'll wait a minute, let me go onstage and let those early arrivals know what's happening. I'll ask if they'll wait." I did. And the response from the venue floor—now about half full, with people still arriving—was a roar of approval.

Kenny Rogers and the First Edition arrived over an hour late. A full crowd was still in the house, antsy but excited.

The band members themselves were incredulous when they finally arrived onstage and the crowd again roared its approval. Kenny Rogers opened the concert with these words: "Wow, who do you think we are, the Beatles?" That brought the house down with screams, yells, whistles, stomping, and clapping. The rafters literally shook.

The concert was fantastic, Kenny Rogers and his group were happy and astounded at their own celebrity, and the concertgoers were thrilled to be part of a memorable show.

How do Kenny Rogers, a concert at a small college, and a better-late-than-never story relate to securing adequate funding for early childhood development?

For nonprofits and citizen activists trying to grow early learning programs, the lesson is this: if you have a star performing for you, lots of people will want to be included in the show.

You want a version of the Beatles, or what people perceive as the Beatles, supporting your efforts. Having star power behind you will exponentially grow the number of willing participants and spike enthusiasm sky-high.

And for large charitable foundations or major corporations in the region with famous names attached, the lesson is this:

Yes, in most communities, you are *the Beatles!*

• • •

Let me take this opportunity to talk directly to major foundations and corporate leaders with star power. I'm speaking on behalf of everyone who desperately believes that we must rethink how we fund early childhood development—that we must make such funding far more robust, and sustainable for far longer periods of time. Here's why I think organizations with star power can lead this effort. (Citizen activists, pay attention: you may need to carry this message to foundations yourself.)

Major players, foundations, and corporate leaders have star power that can bring in large crowds of people who are very happy to be part of a great show. They all want to be at the concert; they all want front-row seats. They are typically willing to lay money on the table to sit near the stage and be associated with philanthropic celebrity. These major players, foundations, and corporate leaders need to be told, "Your star power is real—and it can be leveraged to gain more support from others."

Well-known foundations and corporations and individuals have surprising power to leverage their celebrity status for charitable purposes, by making their full commitment to funding contingent upon matching gifts from the community. Working with a larger number of community partners, "star" organizations have the power to positively influence and institutionalize important efforts such as early learning systems.

I don't mean to be disrespectful to some great charitable foundations that do amazing work (and in fact have helped fund some of my own efforts over the years with large monetary gifts). But if you are a foundation leader, you may have *no idea* how often you fail to leverage your celebrity and bring in other community dollars on a consistent, long-term basis when you make gifts to local programs.

If your charitable foundation has a name in it—like Bill and Melinda, or Buffett, or Allen, or Robert Wood, or Ford, or Packard, or Kellogg, or Koch, or Mortenson, or Bezos, or Annie, or Ellen, or Dolly, or just O, or anything like that—I can tell you right now that you are very likely leaving a lot of other people's money on the table, money that could help achieve and sustain your goals and the community's goals.

In my view as a former local fund and program developer, if you are a person or organization with star power and you truly believe in the community effort you are about to support, it is shortsighted to do so without obtaining some substantial level of local match. That match can come from government, corporations, foundations, or individuals, and it can happen over the long term to institutionalize (sustain) the funding.

You have this power because you are a tremendously credible source. People know your money is real, they respect your well-researched opinion on the issue you've decided to fund, and they know you'll make sure interim progress is measured and reported and that longer-term outcomes are achieved.

State and local policymakers, local corporate leaders, nonprofit leaders, smaller local foundations, and citizens like credible and powerful partners, and they like knowing that those powerful partners have researched the issue before jumping in. And with your "celebrity" assurances attached and with respected local nonprofits executing and marketing the work, chances are they'll be willing to join in at levels you are underestimating. By a lot.

To get specific to the focus of this book, if your goal is to work with communities to start up and then institutionalize support for ECD efforts, let me propose a bold (some will say crazy) vision in the hope that it will stimulate conversation within your organization.

I hope the conversation is not about all the reasons it can't happen, but about what your organization can do to make it happen.

First, let's be honest. Funding an ECD effort is different from many other social projects, because the outcome timeline is so long. We'll see the initial outcomes for a baby born today in five years (readiness for school); follow-up outcomes three or four years after that (third-grade reading proficiency); and even more outcomes several years later, first at the transition from middle school to high school, then at high school graduation.

And finally, the more dramatic, "whole-person performance" outcomes begin appearing in the young adult years, typically between twenty and twenty-five years of age.

And your standing policy is to fund early learning efforts for a year, or three years?

Does short-term investment really make sense in the ECD arena? Obviously not.

And if success in that arena requires more family stability specialists working with far more young children and their families to help provide SAFE and SANE settings, does it make sense to say, "We won't fund that direct service?"

Obviously not.

Is it more important that an ECD effort fit your funding criteria, or that you adjust your criteria to fit the problem?

Frankly, one- , two- , or three-year funding for an ECD design, especially given the decades-long timeline, doesn't make sense to any of us out here working our tails off. Neither does the idea that you won't fund "direct service," when the direct service provided by a family support specialist is perhaps the most vital piece of the puzzle in helping children and their families. We're wondering how we will ever get there, knowing that even key funders are pretty much one and done, providing no direct service funding. It's discouraging. Constantly chasing down resources is terribly time-consuming and exhausting. And I'm pretty sure that's not healthy if you want to advance ECD work as much as we do.

When a key indicator of early learning success is to increase the number of children in SAFE and SANE settings, that means adding direct-service family support specialists (or the equivalent) as a top priority. In that context, a standing policy not to fund direct service obviously isn't very helpful. Sorry, that's just the reality for local workers making near-poverty-level salaries trying like hell to improve their communities by helping families with young children have them ready to succeed in school and beyond.

We've all heard the criticism of for-profit corporations that are driven by quarterly reports, that take their eyes off the horizon and go for short-term payoffs in the form of stock market gains. Is our short-term funding of early learning efforts, which have such long timelines, just as shortsighted?

If we want others at the community level to institutionalize early learning, shouldn't our investments align with our strategies over the long term?

Shouldn't we be thinking of ways to incent a long-term cooperative commitment by local individuals, corporate leaders, foundations, and political policymakers by leveraging creatively structured foundation funds or a major corporate long-term commitment? Of course we should.

Yes, I am suggesting a major commitment of an eye-opening total amount for an eye-opening, groundbreaking duration—*but only if* local funders (government, corporations, foundations, individuals) agree to participate at substantial and sustained levels (consistent with their abilities in any given location). And it's important that organizational policy statements around ECD funding make that long-term commitment clear in both words and action.

For example, what if a major foundation said something like this (purely hypothetical) to a community coalition applying for funds to grow and sustain a robust early learning effort:

"We will fund the recommendations of your community ECD coalition for the next ten years for a total of $20 million.

"As long as agreed-upon indicators and outcomes are being achieved (including more children in SAFE and SANE settings) and our gift is matched (at some given level) by cities and the county and by local corporate leaders, foundations, and community members, we will structure that gift in such a way as to increase the payout annually for the first six years, beginning with $1 million the first year and growing it for the next five years.

"We will continue to fund for the final four years in a partial phasedown to a given sustained amount. But we will do so only if the cities and county and local corporations, foundations, and community members continue to incrementally grow their commitments to sustain this long-term important work (at a certain designated level consistent with the number of children/families to be engaged annually).

"If they commit to this arrangement, we will sustain our funding as long as they do (at some given level). If they aren't on board by that time, if they can't make ECD a priority, then we can't either, and we are out."

Such an agreement not only creates a realistic timeline for institutionalization (a permanent, growing commitment of local sources), but also incents additional local matching funds, encourages policymakers to make the issue a funding priority, *and* gives local organizations the ability to market a headline-grabbing multimillion-dollar challenge match. Your star power, your "being the Beatles," can help nonprofits and other community leaders grow an excited crowd ready to be a part of a big event.

This is no lighter-than-air proposal. I've seen it work (on a smaller scale, obviously); I've helped make it work; and I've witnessed the wide-eyed enthusiasm of policymakers/funders, local foundations, corporate leaders, and philanthropic citizens when such an offer is on the table. In essence, they'll be excited to get to work because they will be bringing your star power and "outside money" to town, they will keep you there for a long while, and they will be publicly associated with you and your record of success. But you should not make it easy for anyone to take your money and run. They need to buy in, understand the importance of and commitment to the effort, and invest in increasing amounts over time.

Your presence will make people sit up and take notice. And it will stimulate them to do things that no one—not you, or they, or the nonprofit community—might have thought possible. If you doubt the truth of that, recall the 2016 presidential primary season, when celebrity made the "impossible" possible.

If I were giving away (investing) millions in a local effort, I wouldn't do it unless my gift was leveraged locally and substantially, in an amount based on local circumstances, into matching gifts from individuals, corporate leaders, foundations, philanthropic citizens, and governments (city, county, and in some cases state). And I'd insist on that match over the long term, to match my own long-term commitment to institutionalizing a priority programmatic effort.

Your partners in the effort—local early learning advocates and program administrators and nonprofit CEOs—should (and would probably be happy to) carry this message to community leaders, policymakers, and funders, in an enthusiastic "look what a great opportunity we have" way. Thus they become your fund developers, as well as their own.

Making complex coordinated systems work is a job in itself, and developing a start-up (if that's where the community is) is a job in itself. And in the case of early learning, creating SAFE and SANE environments in more and more homes takes time, often several years of work with distressed families. Then, reaching the number of new families necessary to hit critical mass with trained staff takes even more time. Together, these things always take more time than we think. Anyone reading this who's worked on a cooperative venture, or in complex systems, or on a start-up, or to expand a program knows exactly what I'm talking about.

But please, let's be realistic about reaching the tipping point—getting effective community-based ECD to the thousands of children who need it. It's going to take a lot of money and much longer than one to three years. We need to get serious if we're going to break through and move beyond the status quo.

Nonprofit leaders spend upwards of 75 percent of their time fundraising just to maintain basic services. In the case of ECD, this is critical time they should be spending to make the system work better and go further. But short-term grants to address long-term goals force them into constant campaigning.

Early in the process of coalition building, of course, it makes sense and is necessary to spend time advocating for funding by making a solid case to the community; this also builds hope and momentum among potential partners. The same applies to funding efforts linked to gaining early community support through matching cash. But these activities should not consume upwards of 75 percent of their time every single year, year after year after year.

Time should be spent instead on collaborative work—program development (learning and adjusting, measuring and improving); cooperation and communication with community partners; and improved and additional direct work with families and children.

Members of Congress provide a good analogy (we all cringe in unison). There is a reason Congress has a 17 percent approval rating: it spends massive amounts of time on fundraising and campaigning and relatively little on deep policy analysis, listening and learning (as evidenced by our many laws with unanticipated consequences). Most members of Congress don't even have the time to read bills before voting on them. Why should we—why *would* we—force our local ECD heroes to operate the same way?

Expecting significant progress from short-term funding is unrealistic in early childhood development, and in some ways it's self-defeating. This model requires small nonprofits to constantly fundraise, just like members of Congress. It is imperative that we rethink policies around the funding of early childhood development.

Fund long-term efforts for the long term. Then through your local ECD partners, who can position the effort as the great opportunity that it is, require local leaders to do the same in order for your "outside money" to come into their town! Those local partners should and can make a compelling case to raise the local money. You (the foundation or grant maker) don't have to do it, and I'm pretty sure you don't want to. You want to see that local commitment at work from the get-go, inspired by your gift but brought to life by your local partners, who can line up local fund-matching commitments.

And a final really important thought: What if you joined forces with other major foundations or grant makers and all three or four (or more) of you kicked in a large annual commitment over ten years for local ECD collective impact coalitions . . . and then *challenged state and federal lawmakers to do the same to match your combined commitment?* This issue, early childhood development, deserves that kind of dramatic action and level of support. It would serve as a newsworthy eye-opener to raise awareness.

And what if the money would not go to another huge bureaucracy, but to highly credible community-based nonprofits or regional coalitions that already distribute funds, require outcomes, do evaluations, and report out success, and with whom you have already worked? There is absolutely no reason to reinvent another bureaucratic wheel.

A collective impact coalition of ECD funders, whose donations are matched by federal, state, and local governments following advocacy work by major organizations with star power, could help change the direction of the nation. We'll explore this idea in more depth in the next chapter. The strategy is difficult—but not impossible. And if we make both funding and implementation work on a large scale by "keeping it small" (see the next chapter), it will likely save *trillions* of taxpayer dollars over time.

Crazy? Maybe. But remember, in an earlier chapter I was the guy suggesting that Ivanka Trump and Hillary Clinton could stun the country by partnering to expand ECD efforts as a national priority. Getting crazy might actually be a good idea.

Now let's shift gears in our effort to get to eighty-eight miles per hour.

Having previously talked directly to potential funders with star power, I'd like to offer a few tips to my colleagues in community-based nonprofits who constantly have to fund-raise to do their great direct-service work in early learning and family stability. Here are some lessons I learned about asking for money over thirty-plus years in the business:

- **Make people sit up and take notice.** Be passionate. Be loud, in a friendly kind of way. Be bold. Be aggressive. Kids' lives depend on it; your own embarrassment or minor discomfort pales in comparison to the important outcomes you hope to achieve. Go out on that limb.
- **On the whole, nonprofit leaders are too damn timid.** Not in programming, but in asking for big commitments. I was that way, too, for quite some time. My biggest professional regret is not being consistently bolder with local foundations and corporations in going after the big bucks and asking for longer time frames to help institutionalize funding for ECD. If you are in just one corporate or political office a week telling the important story of early learning and asking for help, you'll soon have fifty knowledgeable corporate leaders and politicians ready to join the battle. We nonprofit leaders don't do this well, and that weakness hurts us badly. So, grow your own garden of influential champions. Tend that garden constantly. Start taking people to lunch and sharing the research on brain development and explaining what you and your collaborating partners are doing about it. Ask for people's attention first and their understanding second, then ask about their own childhood memories or about their children, then ask for their support for the issue, perhaps asking them to become an advocate with you. *Then* ask for money, once you have earned that right. That could be months or even years later. What are you waiting for?
- **Try to leverage everybody, all the time.** Ask, "If I can get a commitment from them to do this, will you do this?" If you get two (or three, or four) people to say, "Yes, I'll do that if they do that," you've just leveraged successfully.

Getting people to say yes to help leverage their *potential* gift into a greater amount is often easier than getting them to say yes to a straight ask for their cash. Then you return to them with the good news that two or three others have all agreed, and their commitment has been leveraged before they've given you any cash.

- **Ask big.** Corporate leaders think big, and a little ask makes them think it's not all that important. I know this is true of many corporate leaders, because they are visionaries and risk-takers. That's how they got where they are. Ask so big that you shock them. If they aren't shocked, you didn't impress them yet and they won't remember you. They may say, "No, I can't do that much," but that's your opening: "Well, I know I asked a lot; what's more doable for you?"

- **Big money helps raise other big money.** Challenge matches from celebrity foundations open people's eyes and wallets. See my previous message to foundations with star power. Those potential stars have a big role in making it rain more money if nonprofits seriously work the "challenge match" angle.

- **Begin an ongoing conversation about how we fund ECD.** Have serious discussions with major foundations about changing their thinking regarding how they fund early learning. Ask for a meeting *just* to do that. Don't ask for any money. Just ask them to reconsider how they fund long-term efforts with short-term grants—a *very* inefficient method for all concerned. Let them know you understand all the reasons it might be difficult, but you are urging them to think seriously about how to get beyond those traditional one-, two-, or three-year roadblocks to do important work that needs ten-to-fifteen-year horizons. Ask them to have an internal discussion about it—not about why they can't do it, but about what they would have to do to make it happen. Early learning requires committed long-term funding. Period.

- **Always make a case for long-term funding, even if you're sure you won't get it.** Ask specifically for long-term funding, because it's crazy to ask for one, two, or three years when we all know we're talking about a ten-to-fifteen-year time frame for the most powerful early learning indicators and outcomes to present themselves. Over time, repeating this mantra may sink in for them.

- **Promise and deliver strong indicators of progress.** Do it well, do it consistently, do it on time, and do it with funders, politicians, corporate champions, organizational partners, citizen contributors and volunteers, and participating parents. Also, be honest about lessons learned and changes you've made as you've learned some of those lessons. This is a major issue in effective advocacy. Fail to honestly and consistently report out, and you have dug your own grave. Succeed and your story will get bigger and better as you report successes or, in some cases, failures—lessons learned, adjustments made, and new indicators that you are on the right track.

• **BUT (and it's a big one, just like the letters indicate) do *not* compromise your indicators.** In other words, deliver real data about more SAFE and SANE homes, and more kids being successfully reached, and share the indicators that prove it. More meetings are nice, more partners are nice, more trust between partners is nice, more great stories about people feeling connected are nice, and all those things are important. But if you aren't measurably stabilizing more families and helping to lower stress in those families, and if you aren't measurably helping more and more kids have positive, stimulating, brain-growing experiences, then you just aren't there yet.

With the money issue addressed to some degree, let's move to other issues that have the potential to cause dysfunction in collective impact efforts.

CHAPTER 22

Making ECD Work: Mind the Gap

STEP NINE: MISSTEPS AND MINEFIELDS IN COLLECTIVE IMPACT COLLABORATION

We're going to take another brief trip through Great Britain, but we'll stay off the motorway this time, as we've already encountered enough trouble there. Instead, we'll take the London Underground.

The subway system is quite nice in London. It even warns you not to trip as you step from the platform onto the train. The phrase is written right there on the walkway: "Mind the Gap."

That's a fair warning to keep in mind when working to establish a collective impact coalition. Mind the gap: don't be afraid. Just be careful.

FSG has done a remarkable job of outlining many of the difficulties faced by collective impact coalitions and how to overcome them. I again urge community leaders considering a collective impact approach to pay close attention to FSG's work.

After years of personal experience and hard knocks developing and working in large collaborative groups across differing systems (nonprofits, health departments, school districts, and federal and state programs), I've learned several lessons, many of which closely parallel FSG's findings, although I put them somewhat differently:

- **Stay vigilant against mission drift.** The main focus of a collaborative effort is usually aligned with that of most of its member organizations, but not precisely; it requires constant effort and communication to maintain sharp focus on the commonly agreed-upon mission. The group mission must be concise and powerful. Visionaries in the group should use it as a constant reminder of "why we are here," when in fact all the members also have their own mission-specific work to do. They could say, for instance, "We are here to jointly achieve the goal of being among the best early learning communities in America, helping to measurably increase SAFE and SANE family and secondary-care settings for more and more children zero to three years of age." If the case does not remain compelling or is not constantly referenced, members will drift away.

- **Remember that coalition members are essentially volunteers.** Typically, they are not paid for time spent away from their funded mission, even for work that's closely aligned with it. For example, the main mission of their organization may be providing housing, nutrition, or health care for distressed families—closely related to ECD, but not an exact fit. Their volunteer time on the coalition must be honored and respected. This is one of the early sacrifices of collective impact organizations, starting without what FSG calls the "precondition" of adequate funding. Nearly every member of the coalition is sacrificing some time away from their central mission to make the coalition work for young children and the community. My own experience suggests that the FSG precondition of adequate funding is not set in stone, and that a reasonable possibility of funding "if we work together toward it" is enough of a precondition to begin.

- **Constant communication is vital.** While small partnerships or agreements are common among community-based nonprofits, large, sustained, formal collaborations among multiple agencies are rare. There will be lots of surprises for everyone involved, negative as well as positive. Keep talking.

- **Be flexible.** Collaborative efforts often require partners to adjust their processes in order to improve the efficiencies of the larger effort and move it forward. This takes time, trust, and often money (in terms of staff time spent, and/or allowing for small inefficiencies in a partner organization's administrative structure to make the collaborative effort more efficient). For example, if it's common practice at one member organization to ask for a boatload of information in order to process a request from other organizations, it may be asked to forego part of that information to simplify the process for all.

- **Pay attention to the concerns of smaller partners.** Even after committing to the collaboration, they are often concerned about the power of larger partners to drive the agenda without regard for (or knowledge of) the consequences to the smaller organizations.

- **Keep the funding momentum going.** If there is no credible vision for how future funding might be obtained to achieve the coalition's goals, and if there is no work occurring toward securing essential funding, passion and participation in the group will wane. If the right targets for advocacy are selected, an advocacy plan can be both an action plan and a means of providing realistic hope for future fiscal support.

- **Always have an agenda.** If group meetings fall into the common habit of round-the-table reports of "here's what we are doing in our agency," with no specific agenda and little obvious connection to how the report is advancing coalition work toward the overall goal, participation will wane.
- **There must be independent staffing to help coordinate coalition work.** It is too burdensome to permanently hand off to someone with another full-time job. On an interim, start-up basis, however, using staff from member organizations can succeed with some sacrifice. How to structure coalition-specific staffing in the start-up phase is a major issue, and how to transition to a small, independent administrative structure after a certain level of coalition success or growth should be reviewed on a systematic basis.
- **Respect boundaries when it comes to fundraising and volunteers.** Take care not to step on the toes of organizations when it comes to fundraising or the use of volunteers who have been brought to the table in good faith by an agency as potential community champions. Siphoning off either funds or volunteer labor from participating organizations will sabotage the overall effort. Additional gifts are most welcome, of course, but just redirecting a gift at the expense of a nonprofit coalition member is suicide.
- **Measuring and reporting are critical.** Everyone in the collaboration must agree to measure and report data in some similar way, and in a timely fashion, through the "lens" of the collaboration. This work is complex, time-consuming, and typically frustrating for the staff of member organizations, particularly because many of their independent funders require specific data provided in a specific way, too.

  Measuring readiness and other progress indicators and reporting them with consistency across all the collaborating organizations, is a place where collective impact often goes off the rails. Yet it is one of the most important things that must be done for effective future advocacy and transparency. We'll discuss this issue in a bit more depth later.

The overall message here is that collective impact community coalitions can be effective, but they take work. The work will prove to be worth it if sustainability can be achieved, and that requires its own special skill. We'll address that next.

CHAPTER 23

Making ECD Work: Effective Advocacy

STEP TEN: BEING THE BOY SCOUTS

This chapter is about the importance of being prepared and effective messaging when you're talking with politicians and others about ECD. The obvious connection between the preparation issue and the title of this chapter is the famous Boy Scout motto: "Be Prepared."

But first I'd like to talk about a movie entitled *Dave*.

That's a little curveball in the conversation, but we'll get back to the preparation and communication issues in a second.

In the movie *Dave*, a man who works at a temporary employment agency is the spitting image of the president of the United States. He moonlights as a presidential impersonator at parties, conventions, and other venues.

As it turns out, the real president and his handlers need an impersonator to fool the press so the president can go one way while the press goes the other. Dave is hired to do this high-level impersonation. Unfortunately, while he's on the job, the real president has a stroke. Dave is thrown into a situation (again, by the handlers) where he's asked to impersonate the president for an extended period of time.

The part of the movie I like best is when Dave, the fake president, has to find money to save a childcare center, a favorite cause of the real president's wife. Challenged to find a huge amount to cut from the current budget, Dave calls in his longtime friend Murray, an accountant, and they spend the night talking about what should really be a priority and what's really just pork.

Fortunately, there's plenty of pork in the budget—both in the movie and in real life. (And this pork is not a reference to "The Three Little Pigs." That's a different chapter of this book.)

Which is another way of saying—we are now creeping back into the communication area—that when you hear politicians say "there's no money" for sustained ECD funding, what they really mean is that there's plenty of money, but you haven't made a compelling, crystal-clear case why early learning is the most important thing they can do with it—plus there's no substantial support for it. (Let's admit it, going out on a limb alone is not an exciting prospect for most politicians.)

So, don't get lost in that translation. There's money. It's just not yours . . . *yet*.

When you're talking to politicians about money—that is, about our tax dollars, which they're deciding how to spend—you're on delicate ground. I've done it a number of times and learned that lesson the hard way. I'm trying here to spare you some pain, save you some time, and hopefully gain you some ground in the battle for early learning priorities.

Before proceeding, though, I want to take another little detour and suggest that tax dollars should only be a *part* of the finance plan, not *the* finance plan. They have to be a part of the finance plan because in order for us to reach the massive number of distressed children in our communities (who can be turned into successful contributors and save us all a lot of money), everyone has to be in the game. That includes government, which I define as all of us working together on priorities for the common good. Chapter 10, about the costs of a national ECD effort, makes that perfectly clear.

But there's a lot to do before you walk into a legislative office (or any other office) and ask for money. If you haven't made the right preparation, you will suffer the consequences. Whether you're male or female, it's time to "be prepared" like a Boy Scout. If you've convinced your big regional foundations to be "the Beatles" (revisit chapter 21 for a reminder about star power); and your community is reenacting the cavalry, saving the day; and you come prepared, as the Boy Scouts suggest, you are on your way to substantial progress.

Let me share with you my top ten persuasion/advocacy lessons, again, to be prepared and to avoid getting lost in translation.

Lesson 1: Do your homework. And do it on time (in this case, plenty early). By homework, I mean know which politician or corporate executive you are talking to, know the issues they are most interested in, and know their political philosophy and big-picture priorities as best as you can. Know if they have children or grandchildren. Of course, know your stuff about early childhood development, brain development, poverty and stress, family stability, how ECD drives positive outcomes for all, and so on. And know your local numbers, such as how many children need help in your community. Be prepared.

Lesson 2: Prime the pump. The first time you talk to your legislators about the importance of early learning isn't the time to ask them to make it a funding priority. If at all possible, talk to them about it on their home turf first—in their district, not in the office of a government building. Do it in a way that you are offering them important knowledge and your expertise on this issue, with a promise to keep them updated on progress in their (and your) community. When you make that first phone call, say something like, "I'm calling for an appointment with the representative to discuss an issue that's gaining important traction in our community. I'd like to update her on why it's so important here in the district, the current issues on the table, and what her constituents might be asking her about it." It would be helpful to have another constituent with you who can add some real-life knowledge—for example, a kindergarten teacher who can talk about the unprepared kids she sees entering her classroom.

Lesson 3: Make yourself indispensable, a trusted resource on local issues. Offer yourself up as someone who can provide your legislators with helpful answers if issues come up in your "area of expertise" of early childhood development or be able to connect the legislator to others on local issues. Become a reliable source for quick and accurate information—and update your legislators quarterly on your initiative. Be valuable by being knowledgeable and a good communicator. (That means listening as well as talking; find common ground.)

Lesson 4: Get to know the staffers. The people who work in your representative's office can facilitate your access if they know you and know you'll respect their time. They can often be purveyors of important information you want to get to the representative. Know how long they've had the job, whether they think it's interesting, where they went to school, and whether they live in the district themselves. The more they feel connected to you, the better your chances of communicating with the legislator at critical times.

Lesson 5: Connect your conversation to their goals and language. For conservatives, that's often language about cutting social costs, getting good return on investment, improving economic standards and making business more successful, improving our schools, and obtaining proven outcomes. For more liberal politicians, the previous arguments carry weight, and they are also more inclined to respond to ideas such as building strong families, creating family stability, creating successful kids, ending the cycle of poverty, and supporting single moms with kids. Different terms speak more loudly to different people, yet they can be equally correct.

Lesson 6: Create a coalition of messengers. Don't be the only one from the community who talks to your representative about this issue. They need to have the sense that this issue is resonating in their community organically—not through coordinated messaging. Of course, the messaging only needs to *appear* uncoordinated; planning and local coordination among peers is usually a good (and powerful) thing. But that means you must actually *have* a functioning coalition. You all must actually *know* and regularly discuss the data about local indicators of success and outcomes for families and children; you must actually *have* data about your own community; and you all must *know* the things that you have decided collectively are the coalition's highest priorities for advocacy. This is where your corporate champions can be very important, representing a business view. Be prepared. If you are all delivering the same message to your representative, independently and at different times, you have multiplied your power and moved your issue *way* up the list.

Lesson 7: Build legislative momentum. Make sure your representative knows that other politicians, especially those in their party, are also interested in, considering, or supporting this very issue. Political movement is a game of numbers to reach a majority, and politicians need to feel that there is momentum they can build on to reach a majority consensus, rather than having to make it all happen themselves. If you are part of a statewide association, and all the members commit to talking to their representatives, you're on track to building momentum. The same holds true in your city or county: if other nonprofits cover some representatives and you cover others, they will all get covered and hear similar information, and suddenly you might be in a position to create legislative momentum.

Lesson 8: Be patient. Expect development of support to take time; start working on it long before you need anything. Stay comfortably present, consistent, and informed, both on your representative's home turf and on their legislative turf in more formal settings.

Lesson 9: Go big. After laying the initial groundwork, ask big, ask early, ask often, and have others do the same. If you don't treat ECD as a big, important issue, neither will your legislators. (This lesson, like many of the others on this list, also applies to your discussions with corporate leaders and foundations.)

Lesson 10: Get key community support. Other members of your community, including major corporate leaders and your local paper's editorial board, must understand and support your message. You must take the time to make them aware of the importance of the issue and supportive of your efforts to advance it. In fact, you might ask them to join you on occasion when you speak to the politician in question.

In that regard, a main task in building local support is making an annual presentation to several important audiences. Those include the local Rotary Club, Chamber of Commerce board of directors, economic development board, newspaper editorial board, and the executives of local foundations. In each case, this annual effort should be a reminder of what brain science tells us about the long-term value of ECD, a reminder of what's being done in your community to respond to the importance of early learning *as it relates to them*, and a report on your progress—and *not* a request for money. The job is to build understanding, to build stronger relationships, and to build support for the work *as it relates to their work and their goals.* It's easy to let this task slide, but if you do, you're making a huge mistake. Your corporate advocates will grow from these presentations, and as most of us are aware, that corporate leadership can be powerful.

For reading this far on the Top Ten list, you now get an important bonus, an extra "lesson learned" specific to legislative presentations:

Lesson 11: Grab their attention. If you are making a presentation or testifying on the issue of early learning in front of a legislative body, you must *first* get their attention.

Most of the legislators will be looking down, writing something, or maybe thinking about the big donor coming to visit them later in the day, or something other than your presentation. Be creative. Don't bore them with statistics. Tell a story that captures the essence of how important the issue is. *Then* give them data.

I once opened a testimony this way:

"I'd like to tell you about my last Thanksgiving dinner."

Then I stopped talking until every legislator looked up, wondering what would come next. And then I told them the Thanksgiving dinner story I shared earlier in this book, about grandson Phoenix and building a strong foundation.

I opened a legislative testimony a year or two later with the phrase, "I'm here to tell you about what I learned from worms." And I waited until they all looked up, wondering what the heck was next. Then I told them the story about Hector, the "Doctor of Wormology," also related earlier in this book.

Ten years later, nonprofit partners and legislators who were at those presentations still talk with me about them.

Be creative. Tell a story. Start with an opening line they don't expect. Use the story to make a central point. Get them to look up and pay attention. *Then* give them important data.

CHAPTER 24

Resistance on the Home Front

THE EMPIRE STRIKES BACK

I read an interesting article the other day on the website of my hometown newspaper. It was about how a long-established local church had to close its doors due to dwindling participation, but then after much effort, a new early learning program had blossomed in the building. As a result, very young children who lived in the area had an early learning site nearer their homes. Previously, those kids had to be taken by their working parents to a site so far away that it was in a different school district, housed in some vacant but not-very-nice buildings.

Included in the article about the new site was a very positive overview of the types of activities in which the children were participating. By stimulating learning in cognitive areas, social interaction, and emotional development, the program was helping prepare these children for success later in school. Much of this work was facilitated by nonprofit professionals working with the children in partnership with their parents, to help the parents become their children's first, best, and most important teachers.

Overall, it seemed to me an uplifting article, so I thought I'd leave some positive feedback.

After clicking through to the comments section, I was pleased to see that another reader had beat me to it—pleased, that is, until I saw what the other reader wrote.

Let me just quote the public comment as it was written (and spelled):

After 125 years yet another Church of Christ is shut down and turned into a government ran education center. The youth will no long learn about the Torah, Gospel or Prophets but instead be brainwashed into becoming obedient workers for the corperations and the military.

Congress shall make no law respecting an establishment of religion, or prohibiting the free exercise thereof

The state has no right to shut down churches preaching about Jesus Christ and remodel them into re-education centers.

As anyone who knows me might guess, this comment prompted a reply from me. Here's an abbreviated version:

You haven't the faintest clue what you are talking about.

Not very diplomatic, I admit.

Later it dawned on me that when I had two very young kids, I didn't know much about early learning, either. Most of us don't, I suppose. That's one reason so many young parents are nervous. We all want to do the right things, but we're not sure what those right things are.

So here's what we know about doing the right thing for our very youngest children:

Early learning is first about brain development (*not* "brainwashing") from ages zero through three; then ages four through five (Head Start or pre-K and kindergarten and ready for school); then ages six through eight (including reaching third-grade reading proficiency). It is an effort to have as many synapses connected to neurons before the unused or rarely used synapses begin to atrophy. It is literally a race against time to get to Great by Eight.

The most neglected, and perhaps most important, of these time frames is zero through three. This is when huge amounts of brain development and learning can occur to have the child "ready" for preschool and kindergarten.

Early childhood development is also about the parent(s) and other caregivers creating a positive environment in which their young child can thrive, learn, and develop to full capacity. Successful development is most often due to the parent being the child's first, best, and most important teacher in a positive, low-stress, relatively stable environment.

When primary and secondary caregivers can't provide that kind of stimulating environment, an ECD system is how a community can help them, mostly through existing locally based nonprofit and collaborative organizations, by creating its own Mayberry to surround and support young kids.

With the assistance of these community-based organizations, caregivers of all kinds can learn how to provide excellent developmental care for very young children.

And as we discussed earlier, early learning is *not* just about the ABC's and 123's. Those things are an important *part* of the early learning picture, but only a part. In the early years, cognitive development is important, certainly, but research is suggesting that social and emotional development (often learned through both structured and unstructured play) is equally or perhaps even more important for children to succeed in school and later in work, with the ability to coordinate and cooperate effectively with others.

It hardly seems worth repeating—except for the fact that we've all heard the conspiracy theories that "they" are "trying to brainwash our kids"—that early learning is most definitely *not* about putting children in "a government ran education center" where they "can be brainwashed into obedient workers," as our sadly uninformed writer above suggested.

That's just nonsense. Whoever wrote that certainly has a right to their own opinion, but it's an uneducated opinion, and it's wrong.

If we fail collectively to create these formative environments for our communities' young children, or if we simply pass the problem off as "someone else's bad decisions" or "not our job" or reject the idea of community-based ECD as "just another social program," it's highly likely that many of our children will continue to fail. And so, too, will our country. And like it or not, that failure will continue to negatively impact everyone's pocketbook, including yours and mine.

When our children fail, they suffer. And we suffer in multiple ways, including poor school outcomes across the land; a poorly prepared workforce, resulting in an economy that's less globally competitive; and poor adult outcomes, resulting in higher social costs, such as welfare. That has a familiar ring.

CHAPTER 25

An "Aha Moment" on Facebook

BUILDING ON THE WRONG FOUNDATION: A HOUSE OF CARDS

I have a professional colleague, now retired, who goes by the nickname Yaz. He lives elsewhere now, but we sometimes keep in touch via Facebook. Yaz is a lot more conservative than I am, and he uses Facebook to pretty constantly post conservative thoughts and ideas, even some of the shaky ones that may have come from some far-off place (maybe Alternative Facts Universe).

Since we are Facebook friends as well as literal friends, I see those posts and often comment, suggesting that he read a certain article or review statistics or other solid research about the issue that he's raised.

For example, if he writes about a state that has decided to increase restrictions on voter registration so that "voter fraud can be stopped," I might do my own research, find out that the incidence of voter fraud is minuscule in that state as well as around the nation (this is a fact), and suggest he read the research on that issue.

We also see eye to eye on a number of things. Obviously that is the case, or we wouldn't be literal or Facebook friends. For instance, we both think "big money" is way too influential in Congress, and that lobbyists hold far too much sway in policy setting, often working for the benefit of their employers at the expense of the American people. Of course, research shows that about 80 percent of Americans believe the same thing, so it should be no revelation that Yaz and I hold that thought in common.

As another example, we both think that gerrymandering to provide "safe" (highly partisan) voting districts for members of Congress is harmful to democracy. Again, most of America agrees, so it's no surprise that Yaz and I do, too.

In short, we have many interesting Facebook conversations. He often thinks I'm crazy; I often think he's crazy. I sometimes think he makes a good point. And vice versa.

Just yesterday, Yaz posted an article on my Facebook page, praising the fact that the state of Mississippi was now "forcing" (the word used in the headline) people on welfare to do cleanup work in their communities in order to continue to receive benefits. My first thought was, *Didn't they used to do that with criminals and chain gangs?*

But an opposing thought also entered my head: *Well, they are getting money, so I guess asking them to work to get the benefits isn't a totally ridiculous idea.* I couldn't decide in my own head how to respond to Yaz's post.

Then I looked at the picture that went along with the article—it was mostly young women, working—and I had another thought, my first *aha* moment: While those ladies are out there doing community work to qualify for their benefits, where are their very young kids?

And then I began typing a comment, and here's what I wrote:

I'd much rather have them in parenting classes and ECD classes with their children, so their kids have a fighting chance to end the cycle of poverty and stay off welfare.

Yaz responded this way:

Kids should see their parents work, they already have free everything.

And I fired back:

Yaz, this response floors me. If anyone should know how important early childhood development is to brain development in little children, you should.

And if anyone should know how unprepared some parents are to bring up kids (often due to their own poor backgrounds and uninformed parents), you should.

It has absolutely NOTHING to do with 'free everything' and EVERYTHING to do with kids being ready to succeed because their brains have been stimulated by the right activities at the right time to help them be successful in school, work, and life.

And as you know perfectly well, informed and engaged parents are the child's first, best, and most important teachers. It's brain science.

The conversation above actually created a second *aha* moment for me about our long and frustrating War on Poverty, introduced by President Lyndon Johnson in the mid-1960s. That sudden realization came in the form of a question to myself: *Have we been building our poverty-fighting efforts on a weak foundation? Is the War on Poverty a house of cards— unsteady, likely to collapse every time the economy takes a dive?* We touched on this subject earlier; now let's go a little deeper.

Our emphasis on "ending poverty," whether by progressives or conservatives, has tended to focus on adults living in poverty right now. Much of progressives' thinking appears to be along these lines: people lack housing, we try to provide housing; they lack nutritious food, we try to provide nutritious food; they lack job (or job-seeking) skills, we try to provide that training. And so on.

The conservative mind, in the meantime, often focuses on the adult in the context of poverty and work, poverty and "laziness" stemming from a "sense of entitlement," poverty and bad decision-making, and so on.

For over half a century now, the focus of our War on Poverty has been on adults in poverty right now, and giving them just enough to squeak over the proverbial "poverty line" so we can take them off the books and declare victory.

The kids in those families? Well, they're along for the ride through no fault of their own, so we'd better keep them housed and fed.

In the same way that we've been blaming public schools for our children's failure to learn, are we missing the obvious in our War on Poverty and fighting on the wrong battle-field? To get to the root of our children's learning failures, we had to look to the children's past, before school, and the role of the parent. Here, we are again questioning the proper role of the parent—but the question has to do with our own system's requirements of parents on welfare, and how the role we are requiring them to play might impact their children and poverty in the long run.

Many adults living in poverty grew up in high-stress environments with lots of adverse childhood experiences, just as their own children are growing up now. Many did poorly in school themselves or failed entirely and dropped out. They, too, suffered from a lack of SAFE and SANE settings. Their homes lacked stimulating early activities and experiences, and their brain development suffered as a result. As we know from science, poor early brain development has lifelong consequences for people. Even as they continue fighting to learn and improve, they are often a bit slower in decision-making, perhaps not seeing all options or understanding the consequences, just like Dan and me on the English roundabout. But the consequences of their mistakes are far worse than having to pull over to the side of the road and scaring a little English lady while doing so.

Are these folks permanently disabled? No. But like our story of driving in England on the "wrong" side of the road, they are going to struggle in the roundabouts and maybe run themselves (and others) off the road a few too many times as they learn. Eventually, they will get there, but the travel will be slower and the expense higher. And if the economy or something else goes south on them, there's a high chance they'll end up right where they started.

As we discussed about other types of interrupted brain development—for instance, with a stroke—over time and with great effort, new brain pathways, decision pathways, can be built. Many of these parents have gone through enough adverse life experiences that they've likely built alternative pathways to deal with them. But while they've been learning through hard knocks, their children are going through those adverse experiences, too.

For the children, those adverse experiences are piling up. Their stress levels are high and their brain development is slowed, even while some of those same experiences, processed at the adult level, are creating learning opportunities that help their parents survive.

And we have been using that shaky foundation—parents who aren't necessarily prepared to be the best mentors, and who aren't necessarily prepared for the workplace or for the transition to a new kind of workplace—as a starting place for our efforts to end poverty.

Hmmm. What was that my four-year-old grandson, Phoenix, said on Thanksgiving Day about "building on a strong foundation" if we want something to last? Doesn't that lesson apply here? Should we be rethinking our tactics in the War on Poverty?

Studies have found that since Temporary Assistance for Needy Families (TANF) was instituted in 1997, extreme poverty has actually increased. A 2011 study by the University of Michigan's National Poverty Center found that families living on less than two dollars per person a day more than doubled from 1996 to 2011.[55]

Should we be making subtle changes in the War on Poverty to focus on breaking the cycle of poverty by shifting resources toward the accelerated development of children in these families? Shouldn't we be making sure the children don't end up in the same place as their parents?

For example, in the opening to this chapter, I mentioned that Mississippi now requires welfare recipients to do menial cleanup work. What if the state instead required them to attend a series of parenting classes or other learning opportunities focused on early childhood development, perhaps with their child in tow, as part of the "earn your benefits" philosophy? Wouldn't this be a much more useful activity long-term than filling some low-paying, unlikely-to-go-anywhere jobs? Instead of having them pick up garbage, should we ask welfare recipients to participate in organized and well-developed training that will help them become the best parents they can be?

Should we ask that their children be developmentally assessed as part of the exchange for benefits—a quid pro quo we can all live with? We could then use that knowledge to identify the children's developmental needs, and to teach the parents and other caregivers the best activities to engage their kids' minds and prepare them for success. The information can be used to help establish more positive relationships between parents and children. This would create a far better return on investment over the long run.

Should we think of other creative ways to engage welfare parents in skill building to facilitate early childhood success, further increasing the chances of breaking the poverty cycle for future generations?

An article in *Time* magazine explained how a simple tradition such as regular family meals can measurably improve a child's physical health and success in school and life, noting, "Studies have long shown that eating as a family brings with it a cornucopia of benefits, ranging from decreasing a child's risk for obesity, eating disorders, drug and alcohol use, depression and teen pregnancy, to improving their academics performance, eating habits, self-esteem and resilience."[56]

Jerica Berge, director of Healthy Eating and Activity across the Lifespan, at the University of Minnesota, has done several studies specifically on breakfast. She has found that the health benefits of family meals are not dependent on the time of day.[57] Our welfare programs should be helping make this type of basic family engagement more prevalent in young households.

Another example of how we could change the focus to children might be offering more generous housing subsidies for welfare recipients whose very young children are actively participating in developmental programs. We might extend that higher subsidy as long as verified progress is being made toward reaching third-grade reading proficiency, a process that could include the parent regularly reading with the child, participating in the ECD program, and engaging with the child in other developmentally appropriate activities.

Note that I'm *not* suggesting that subsidies for other recipients be reduced, but instead suggesting that a premium of some amount (in health care, nutrition, housing, and other critical areas) be added to families with children ages zero to three in return for their participation in parent-child activities on a scheduled and consistent basis.

This seems to me a policy approach worth careful consideration. Otherwise, we risk the War on Poverty continuing to be built on a house of cards—a shaky structure built on shaky assumptions about what will "win" the war. Assumptions that over fifty-five years have not played out.

At present we are hoping to build a better, sturdier future on a shaky foundation of often ill-prepared parents who didn't receive proper support for full and healthy development themselves. Typically (though not always), they are not well educated or prepared in other important ways. They've learned or are learning through the school of hard knocks. In the meantime, their children lack well-prepared mentors and live in a world full of adverse experiences that are slowing their neural development. By the time they're ten, their unused brain synapses and neurons have begun slowly atrophying, a natural process as one ages.

Shouldn't we focus our welfare efforts more heavily on goals for the children, facilitated through the parents? Shouldn't we "go upstream" and prevent the kids from falling in?

Shouldn't we help welfare parents decrease adverse childhood experiences in the household? Shouldn't we help them create SAFE and SANE places where their children can thrive and grow, with the potential to avoid poverty and become successful adults?

We must still support the parents, of course—make no mistake about that. To be successful with either parents or children, we must provide a more stable environment so that the children have a better chance for developmental stimulation, and educational and then lifelong success. For parents, that stability will often hinge on lowering the stresses related to deficits in income and the family's basic needs; for the children, that improved environment will often mean more positive engagement with parents very early in life, time made more constructive by the mentoring parents receive from ECD staff.

This improved engagement with and for the children can't happen when the parents are out doing menial jobs all day just to receive their benefits.

Economic Mobility Pathways, or EMPath, a nonprofit in Boston, has built its whole service-delivery model around brain science and adult coaching, which it describes in its 2014 report, *Using Brain Science to Design New Pathways Out of Poverty.*[58]

After years of coaching adults and watching those benefits trickle down to children, Tara Mathewson, in a 2017 *Atlantic* article, "How Poverty Changes the Brain," points out that "EMPath has brought children into the center of its model—offering a way out of intergenerational poverty with brain science."[59]

Elisabeth Babcock, the president and CEO of EMPath, noted in the article that people in poverty "tend to get stuck in vicious cycles where stress leads to bad decision-making, compounding other problems and reinforcing the idea that they can't improve their own lives."[60]

Focusing more of our welfare-related efforts on children is a vital difference in approach. It's very likely that if the children receive proper care, they will be better equipped to permanently break the cycle of poverty in their lifetimes, at a far higher rate and with less recidivism, than their parents.

Given the right SAFE and SANE setting, these kids will be ready to respond and succeed no matter the economic circumstances. They will be smarter, more adaptable, more confident, and better able to see more options and make good choices in a timely manner, because their brains will be more fully developed in the early years, when that progress counts the most.

And as we have documented, their success will be a tremendous victory for all of us.

CHAPTER 26

Imagine

A DREAMER? I'M NOT THE ONLY ONE.

I worked on ECD issues for nearly thirty years, helping to form communities far more focused on giving very young children a successful start. Our team did so by making better, more coordinated use of our existing (mostly nonprofit) community resources, advocating aggressively for more resources to assist families, identifying the children who most needed our help, regularly assessing their development in concert with their parents, and then working closely with their families. Our work with families was most effective when they were partnered with family support specialists (or the equivalent)—nonprofit staff trained to help parents or caregivers increase positive engagement with their child. We started a coalition in the early years with a few dreamers—professionals including nonprofit and school leaders and family support workers, as well as parents—and we added many more, hundreds more, turning a dream into reality . . . for a time. You can, too. This chapter will help identify what that actually looks like when it's happening.
   Imagine that.

Child A isn't born yet. Her parents both have low-paying jobs, with a combined income below the poverty line. They have come to the county health department for a prenatal screening, to make sure the pregnancy is progressing safely.

   Fortunately for this family, the health department has won a Nurse-Family Partnership grant (probably a short-term award of up to three years). Through an interview with the parents during the checkup, the department is able to determine whether the family is susceptible to some of the risk factors that create stress and slow child development. If it is, and if the family consents, a nurse is assigned to work with them for the next year to reduce the likelihood of negative outcomes for the baby.

   After a year, and again with the family's consent, the health department uses its established partnerships to connect the family to a local nonprofit (often a community action agency or culturally relevant nonprofit) that helps distressed families. That nonprofit assigns a trained staff member to continue assisting the family, typically in the home. These meetings might focus on parenting skills or similar training, or if things like food or housing assistance are needed, the counselor might help the family navigate those systems to keep the household stable, with lower stress. The staff member is likely also paid through a short-term grant (up to three years).

With the family's consent and the signing of a confidentiality form, community-based work with the family (starting at the health department) is entered onto a spreadsheet stored in the cloud and available only to the partners involved. It's a simple document serving as a single point of entry and information about meeting dates, issues discussed, referrals made, assistance received, indicators of child/family developmental progress, etc. It also keeps the family from having to provide the same personal information every time they are referred to a different source of assistance.

At some point, the family might be referred to the partner children's museum or a partner county library that provides free developmental screenings for young children. These screenings, too, are often done by a nonprofit professional whose work is funded through a short-term grant. Children found to have developmental issues needing attention are referred to another partner in the system who deals with the identified need. In some cases, these may be private-sector professional partners who have agreed to assist with a certain number of cases per year.

As the child grows older, through the ages of one, two, and three, the family support specialist works with the family on early learning tools that are age appropriate (based on best practices) and on parenting skills, so the child continues to advance.

As the child approaches age three, her family and the support specialist contact the local Early Head Start program, to begin the transition to more formal education. The parents continue to participate with the Head Start program and staff, perhaps attending weekly after-work meetings at which food may be served as a special incentive to keep families involved.

When the child is around five or six, the Head Start staff, coordinating with the parents, contact her kindergarten or first-grade teachers—also partners in the consortium through their school district superintendents—to begin a transition to public education. Fortunately, with this kind of transition approach through community-based nonprofits, most children will be ready to learn and succeed when they (and hopefully their parents) meet their kindergarten teacher for the first time.

Child B *enters the system differently, when one of his parents calls 211. This is the local help line, typically administered regionally by a nonprofit. It fields about eighty thousand calls annually from people desperately seeking help, often as a last measure. In this case it's winter, and the family's heat is about to be shut off. During the discussion, the call center staff, a volunteer, learns that the family has a two-year-old. They learn this because the 211-call center is part of the early learning coalition, and so the volunteer asks questions about young children as part of the intake process.*

The call center is funded partly by a state grant but constantly struggles to find other support as it fields a growing number of calls. Nevertheless, the volunteer not only connects the family to a resource for help with heat assistance, but offers to refer the caller to an agency with a family support specialist who might visit with them and connect them to child development resources.

The parent consents and is referred to the helping agency, who then assigns a support specialist to meet with the family, assess their needs, and help them create a positive learning environment for their young child.

In a best-case scenario, Child B receives the same assistance Child A received, with the participation of the parent, followed by a similar transition to Head Start and then to public school.

Child C enters when her parents show up at the local food bank, requesting assistance. As part of the ECD consortium, the food bank first supplies the needed food if it is available—which in this case it is likely to be, as the food bank gives priority access to families with children three and younger—and then asks to meet with the family briefly to assess their situation more fully.

After learning that the family is not yet connected to the ECD system, the food bank requests and receives their consent to refer them to the most appropriate helping agency that incorporates family support specialists (or the equivalent) in its administrative design.

That helping agency assigns them a family support specialist who enters them into the database in the cloud after the family signs a confidentiality agreement. The staff member then continues to work with the family, as in the cases of Child A and Child B.

Here we see that not all nonprofits will have family support specialists as part of their design. In this case, the first-contacted agency, the food bank, has an assessment specialist; that specialist's top priority is to identify families with young children who would benefit from a referral to another nonprofit in the community that does have family support specialists.

A vital key to the success of the community-based model is the constant growth in the number of family support specialists in the system. If this is not happening, it is nearly impossible to add new children and new families into the system.

Child D comes to the attention of the early childhood consortium when his father's employer calls the local United Way. The employer would like someone to come to his business to talk about alcohol abuse and where and how workers can refer someone they know who needs help.

As a result of that request, a presentation at the business is made, and Child D's father is later referred to a nonprofit organization (funded largely by short-term grants) that specializes in drug and alcohol abuse assistance. The nonprofit assesses the family and learns there are two young children in the household. If that agency works with families on parenting skills and improving the overall family environment as well as on the issue of substance abuse, it might assign the family to its own staff. If its staff is focused on substance abuse only, it might refer the family to a local agency for parenting and ECD work with a family support specialist.

Child E *enters the system through a nonprofit with emphasis on the unique issues of a specific population or culture, such as the local Centro Latino or Urban League, a Native American–focused organization, or an English as a second language (ESL) organization. Many of these organizations have family support staff or counseling specialists in their systems. Because in this hypothetical case they have also joined the ECD coalition, they pay particular attention to families with very young children who may be in a high-stress or low-engagement environment (or both). They then either assign the child and family (with family consent) to an internal family stability specialist trained in parenting and child development, or hand off to a trusted partner organization that has such staff. The child and family then begin the same evolutionary process as cases A, B, C, and D—home meetings focused on family and child development; regular progress assessments; a handoff after one or two years to Early Head Start, Head Start, or a similar state-funded effort for years three, four, and five and a transition to kindergarten (or first grade, if the state does not yet have kindergarten). Then the teachers at that level can begin with all their students on a more even playing field, helping them focus on fundamentals so they reach third-grade reading proficiency on time (about eight years old).*

Children F through Z *may similarly come into the system through a variety of means, if, in fact, the community has a strong consortium of partners who have agreed to work together. And in each case, depending on whether the initial-contact organization has appropriate family support staff, it will either assign the family to its own staff and enter data onto a cloud-based document after getting family approval, or refer the family to an appropriately staffed partner organization.*

Initial contact might be made at a women's shelter, a dental program for low-income families and children, a local church, or a local school. If it's made at school or even at the other venues, staff or teachers might learn that some of their struggling students have younger siblings. Or a referral might come from nonprofits with a cultural connection, such as Centro Latino, the Urban League, or an ESL organization. Housing authorities and homeless shelters should obviously be an active part of this picture, as well, and can prioritize assessing and referring families with very young children. Boy Scout and Girl Scout chapters, Boys & Girls Clubs, and YMCA/YWCAs may do the same.

Meanwhile, imagine a consortium leadership group that meets monthly to discuss the strengths they see developing in the system, what needs to change, and what resources are needed as a shared priority. Almost always, two things will be on the priority list: 1) more family support workers added somewhere in the system, as determined by the consortium, and 2) additional resources in food, housing, health care, transportation, or some other significant areas of weakness, depending on the specific community and its needs.

Imagine consistent follow-up with city and county governments, the state legislature, and local foundations, conducted by different members of the local coalition, all singing the same song, advocating for the same vital priority, even if it does not directly improve or impact that member's budget (but still improves the overall service and the number served in the system). That's how power is developed in advocacy work.

Imagine annual presentations to the Chamber of Commerce, the Rotary Club, and the economic development board, and ongoing scheduled visits with the community's key political, corporate, and religious leaders. The idea is to provide them with information that might be useful to them, to remind them why ECD is so important to them and the community, to update them on progress and positive indicators, and to identify how the ECD effort can create even more positive outcomes and what resources are needed to do it. Imagine *them* taking up the agenda of the early learning consortium and making the case with key leaders who decide where funding goes.

Imagine this cooperative effort being held together by a small central staff, with much of the actual family/child fieldwork being done by existing partners with existing administrative systems—no need to build a new bureaucracy. The central staff coordinates the coalition meetings, develops agreements on priorities, keeps the children's progress reports coming regularly, develops advocacy messaging for consistent use by the coalition, and coordinates community presentations (Chamber of Commerce, Rotary, corporations, economic development board, school superintendents, etc.). And instead of year-to-year grants and constant fundraising, which make the other general educational presentations nearly impossible, imagine having a sustaining grant for ten to fifteen years, from a combination of sources and challenge matches, which would free the small coordinating organization to do the vital work of "system organizing."

Now imagine in this system an organization devoted to giving secondary-care providers nearly as much assistance as families receive through their family support specialists. In this case, those being educated and assisted in providing more outstanding developmental care are members of the loose system of childcare providers that exist in almost every community. And imagine that those who make substantial advances are identified, rewarded, and recommended as well-trained childcare providers, giving their business a substantial boost. Imagine that these "star" providers receive some kind of reward for their advanced care, such as new books, developmentally appropriate toys, or a needed piece of furniture.

Training might also be provided to grandparents who take care of young ones while their parents work, or to kindergarten and first-grade teachers who would like to know more about creating positive learning environments for their five-to-seven-year-olds.

All these things can be done. In fact, most of them have been done but not sustained. Because having to rely on multiple sources of short-term funding, all starting and stopping at different times, makes it impossible to cement the system in place and build upon it.

As long as we continue to fund a long-term issue with short-term grants, and as long as we continue to move on to the next "hot issue" of the day and take our eyes and efforts away from early childhood development, we are subjecting our children, our families, our schools, our communities, our nation, and our own pocketbooks to unnecessary negatives.

Frankly, it's time to step up and step out. We have to rapidly increase the number of children in our ECD systems, and if we don't have those systems, we must begin growing them now.

It should have happened long ago.

CHAPTER 27

Blind to Missed Opportunity

ARE WE GOING TO THE PROM?

As a young guy, I was late to the dating game. Really late. Like after-high-school late. And only then did I venture out because my future one and only and current perfect wife of fifty-two-plus years was willing to press the issue.

That's not to say I didn't *want* to date—it's just that I didn't have the guts, didn't know how to talk to girls about that kind of thing, and at the time didn't have a dad I could ask for advice.

And, of course, at sixteen and seventeen, we all had good friends who would kid us with stuff like, "Why should she go out with you when she could have any guy in school?" Even though I knew they were just giving me a hard time, I always suspected there was more than a grain of truth to it.

In other words, I remained a coward when it came to girls in high school.

Which was hard to do, because I had a pretty bad crush on one particular girl. Let's call her Sally. (Well, OK, I also had a crush on a beautiful blonde named Patti and did nothing about that either except mumble incoherently.)

I sat behind Sally in eighth grade. She was dark haired, quiet, and shy. If you've ever seen the classic 1944 movie *National Velvet*, which starred Elizabeth Taylor as a teenager, then you know what Sally looked like in 1960. I had just moved to town and didn't know anyone, so I thought it was a good omen that I was immediately seated behind what must have been the prettiest girl in the school district. Not just the school. The entire district.

Sally hardly ever spoke in school. But I noticed that every time she did say something, it was usually thoughtful and accurate. It was also startling to everyone in class because she spoke up only once every couple of weeks.

After observing her for a couple of months, I finally decided (translation: I finally found the courage) to compliment Sally the next time she made a nice contribution to the class discussion. I really did think it might help her feel more confident and open up a bit. And it didn't hurt that if I tapped her on the shoulder (which I did), she'd have to lean back, turn around, and see what I wanted (which she did). I whispered a strategic but well-intended compliment: "You know, you ought to speak up more often. Every time you do, you say something really smart." She blushed. She said thank you. She turned back around. End of eighth-grade highlights. I had forgotten to plan past Step One.

As the years passed and we progressed to high school, Sally grew more and more beautiful and I grew more and more nerdy. I shot up six inches in one summer between my sophomore and junior year, and then I had trouble walking, talking, and keeping my glasses from falling off for the next two years. Yes, I even had tape on my glasses.

Finally, in my senior year, Sally and I had another class together—two semesters of civics, back-to-back. This time she sat directly behind me. I was coming more into my own, but I still was not very comfortable with girls. Nevertheless, we bantered back and forth and had too much fun talking, until our teacher separated our seats.

As the year progressed, I was faced with the ultimate horror of senior prom. Having never asked a girl out, I was in a panic. Yes, other girls had asked me to Sadie Hawkins dances, when the girls asked the guys—remember, this was the mid-1960s—but me ask a girl? Never!

I started asking my friends if they were going to the prom. Yes, they had asked someone. "Well, what do you think of me asking Sally?" To a person, they looked at me with great skepticism. And that's when the "Why would she go out with you?" phrases entered the discussion. Unwelcome advice, but, I concluded, probably accurate. As a result of my analysis, I never asked her.

In the end, at the very last minute I asked the smartest girl in the same civics class— not unattractive, apparently unattached, a friend, and no threat to my young manhood if she turned me down, because I didn't have a huge crush on her. We had a fun time with friends.

The story, long as it is, doesn't end here.

I had the good fortune of meeting my future wife, Alvarita, the summer after my high school graduation. We worked in the same restaurant, and I fell in love with her the first day we had a thirty-minute lunch break together. Two years into our relationship, I was fully committed to her. We were both going to Eastern Washington State College—I was a sophomore living in a men's dormitory, and she was a freshman in a women's dorm.

One afternoon I was in my dorm lounge and saw a vaguely familiar face walking toward me. As she approached, I could see it was one of Sally's best high school friends, who it turns out knew someone in our dorm and was visiting him. I gave her a friendly "hi" as she walked up, but she was not in a good mood.

"I've been really mad at you for a long time," she responded sharply.

I gave her a look of startled surprise, I'm sure, and said something like, "Why would you be mad at *me*?" I couldn't imagine why, since I hadn't seen her for nearly two years.

She blurted with sincere anger, "Because Sally really was expecting and waiting for you to ask her to the senior prom in high school, and you really, really hurt her feelings by not even talking to her about it. She was really hurt, and you made her cry!"

I was so stunned I could barely reply. A small push would have knocked me off my feet. I'm sure Sally's friend wanted to do just that.

"You've got to be kidding me!" I meekly responded, dumbfounded. It was all I could think to say. Sally's friend spun around and hurriedly stomped away.

Often, missed opportunities are the cause of great and unforgettable regret, and come attached to unfortunate news of other things missed or caused as a result of inaction. It's not often that a great opportunity missed—like not taking Elizabeth Taylor the Younger to the senior prom because you didn't even know she wanted you to—turns into gold. In this case, my missed opportunity did, since I met and fell in love with my future wife just months later.

While in this case regrettable-in-retrospect but not disastrous, some opportunities missed are far more consequential than a missed date with the prettiest girl in high school.

And that's how we transition from a story about going to the prom to a discussion of early learning.

We are blowing opportunities with millions of our very youngest kids. And we are blowing it right now, while you are reading this sentence.

We've been blowing it since the 1980s, when the research on brain development made clear what was happening. Thirty-five years is a long time to be stupid and wrong when the truth is staring you in the face.

If you have older kids, you know the opportunities to reach and teach very young children are fleeting. Those years from zero through three probably seem like another lifetime, they went so quickly. And if you recall your child as a newborn compared to who they were by age three, you'll understand completely how much capacity to learn they actually have. Incredible capacity, in a very short and tremendously important time frame.

For millions of American children, much of that capacity is going unused. Quite often the result is a child lost and, later, an adult adrift.

We can stop that waste to a large degree, and turn millions of children into assets for their communities and our country. Will we?

First, I have a simple message for parents, a little bit of "if I only knew then what I know now" advice. Think of these comments as important things you can do to make the most of those early years with your children.

A BRIEF OVERVIEW OF THE EARLY YEARS FOR PARENTS

My youngest child is now forty. That's relevant only because it means most of what I know about early childhood development and early learning I learned well after he was born. And *that's* relevant because, like most parents of young children, my wife and I had a lot of questions about the "best" and "right" things to do.

Just like any other parents, we had to make a lot of spontaneous decisions—and figure out how to do whatever we decided—in response to our spontaneous child. Let's call it adult learning on the run. Almost all parents are engaged in that same pursuit at some time.

A critical lesson I learned on the run that connects directly to brain science came from reading to my kids when they were very young, just learning to read, and then watching my wife do the same thing. For some reason, they far preferred reading with Mom to reading with Dad. After noticing this, I asked my wife about it.

"You're always trying to help them get the words right, sounding things out, and so on," she said. "I just want them to have fun reading; the rest will come later because they enjoy reading."

She was *so* right. I had turned my reading time with them into a chore, something with a bit more tension and stress. She had turned reading into a fun activity, zipping through stories at a happy pace, not worrying about anything but the story and talking with the kids about it.

After our talk, I attempted to adopt her style, and if the kids came to a word that stumped them, as they often did, we didn't hang there too long—I pronounced the word and we bounced ahead. Yes, we sounded things out later, as they got older, but our early reading time needed to be warm, high engagement, low stress, and fun.

Here are three ways to apply this lesson in the context of ECD and brain science:

Try to keep the stress low. Brain science tells us that lower-stress environments facilitate a child's brain development, while high-stress environments cause chemical reactions that slow brain development. Find ways to keep your kids' environment as relaxed as possible. Life will not be totally stress free, of course, but if you want your children to be well along on the ECD scale when life gets tougher and more complicated, keeping things happy and fun at an early age can go a long way.

Your kids don't know you had a hard day at work. All they know is you are short with them and inattentive. Your kids didn't have anything to do with your mortgage payment or your credit card bill. All they know is that you are mad and things are tense and stressful in your house. Handle those things in private as much as you can, and when your kids are around, be an intentional and positively engaged parent.

Find new ways to have fun together. Brain science also tells us that high-engagement activities help children's brains grow new synapses and connect neurons in new ways through new experiences. Repeating these activities helps hardwire those brain pathways. You and other caregivers should be doing what you can to give them varied experiences, with some repetition, in fun, low-stress ways.

Be a good mentor regarding social and emotional skills. We know from research that social and emotional development at an early age has a high correlation to later success in school and then in life, even after twenty-five years. That means things like learning to play well with others, share, collaborate, understand boundaries, and communicate well (listen and understand as well as talk and write), are very important to later success. This is why the phrase *play to learn* has so much relevance these days.

It is often stated that the parent is a young child's "first, best, and most important" mentor. The list of "good-parent" tips is long, and there are many sources for concrete examples. But if you keep those three simple, general concepts in mind, they will prove useful as you dare to be a parent and, beyond that, strive to be a good one. Becoming a parent is pretty easy; being a good one is a bigger challenge.

For those who simply don't see a role for themselves in this effort, they may be asking, "Why should I get involved?" Or perhaps thinking, "It's so discouraging to see so many who need help."

This very issue popped up just yesterday, as I was talking to one of my doctors during a routine checkup.

We were discussing a mutual friend who had just had a baby very early, in an emergency situation. I had seen her only weeks before, and she'd been happy and pregnant. Fortunately, both mom and child were OK, but I mentioned to my doctor that on my last visit with our pregnant friend, she and I had had a fifteen-minute conversation about early childhood development.

My attending doctor surprised me by becoming a bit sullen and saying, "It's sad, isn't it? It's so tough for kids today. And there are so many parents who don't know what they are doing." Her look and tone said, "I'm not very optimistic."

I gave her a shorter answer than the one that follows here, but in essence, it was a positive one.

Well, yes, it is the parents' job to raise their children to succeed. And yes, many of them are failing at that job, to a large degree because they, too, had lots of adverse childhood experiences that impacted their own development. They lived in high-stress environments themselves; their parents may not have been very intentionally engaged with them, either.

Their experiences were likely limited, too. It's quite likely they were limited by their own families' economic circumstances and by stress that negatively impacted their brain development. In other words, they learned (and many are still learning) the hard way, with bumps and bruises from running off the metaphorical road a few times. As a result, many can't be effective mentors without some guidance. And that's why this problem is a cycle, repeating from one generation to the next.

The good news is that most parents, no matter their individual situation, want their kids to succeed. In my experience they are open to guidance when approached with respect and a common goal (their child's success) in mind. They will, for the most part, gladly participate in the effort to have their children Great by Eight.

And that's where the community of nonprofits and others—the entire village—can step in to help.

Where Progressives Are Missing the Boat: Unfortunately, *progressives* are missing an opportunity. They need to be talking about how to build strong children into contributing adults, or at least move in that direction, to end the cycle of poverty.

They should be talking about the payoff for *all* of us when ending the cycle of poverty happens at a grand scale as a result of early childhood development—taking the long-term view. They need to talk to their political opponents and show them, in the *opponents'* terms, why and how early childhood development would benefit them and *their* goals.

But they can talk about this prospect only if advancing ECD as a primary anti-poverty weapon is what most social services are designed to do. Instead, most social services are focused on reducing immediate poverty among adults, and those efforts are only marginally successful.

Our welfare system is *not* laser focused on creating SAFE and SANE environments for kids, working with parents to develop great parenting skills, and stopping the cycle of poverty long term by turning the children into successful graduates, workers, and citizens. Great by Eight needs to get on the agenda. Adjusting our welfare focus to this different set of priorities would have a much higher likelihood of stopping generational poverty than our current War on Poverty, which is still being waged with 1960s "philosophical weaponry" after more than half a century.

Prioritizing ECD would refocus our tactics. We should focus on the development of the youngest kids in distressed or impoverished settings. And we should systematically, continuously engage parents in that process in exchange for them receiving taxpayer-supported social services for stability.

We know the details about brain development in children make people sit up and listen.

We know the details about neurons and synapses beginning to atrophy at around age ten make people sit up and listen.

We know the idea that we are in a race against time to create positive environments for kids, before we lose them to slow development, makes people sit up and listen. Great by Eight sells and inspires.

We have to lay out the details of this case, over and over, and by doing so change the narrative about how to end the cycle of poverty and change the current systems that work only marginally.

I know these details make people sit up and listen and respond enthusiastically, because I've seen it repeatedly. I've spoken on this issue to very large groups, many times. There are always lots of yeses from the audience, lots of nods of agreement, lots of ovations, lots of people wanting more details after the speech. Many adults have kids. They get it, they've seen the incredible growth in their own children, and they understand the vital importance of the early years because they've experienced it.

We have more than fifty years of conclusive proof that we aren't going to win the War on Poverty simply by giving more and more money to housing programs, nutrition programs, mental health programs, health programs, welfare programs, and so on, until every adult is "on an even playing field" and reaches self-sufficiency on a false path of marginal jobs paying minimum wage. In good economic times, these folks are technically "out of poverty" and our poverty rate looks better. But the minute the economy slows, the house of cards collapses.

I would again suggest that those adult-centered approaches have proven to be marginally effective at best, and not affordable on the grand scale we must achieve to say we've made a permanent dent in the poverty rate.

But we *can* win the War on Poverty if we focus on the other end of the family spectrum: the children. We need to commit to ensuring that every child develops to their capacity while living in a SAFE and SANE environment and engaged with knowledgeable caregivers. Parents are critical to that design.

The basic need for stabilizing services to these economically distressed families may not change. But our focus on why they need them, and what we ask parents to do in return, must change. Rather than having them work low-skill, low-paying jobs, we should have them participate in structured activities that are child oriented, with a focus on parenting skills, positive engagement, and SAFE and SANE settings. A phrase being used today is that we've got to Build Back Better. If we apply that philosophy to our War on Poverty by refocusing it on ECD, the potential benefits to the country will be huge.

Why Conservatives Should Hop On Board: *Conservatives*, too, are missing an enormous opportunity by not promoting early childhood development as a major strategy to facilitate economic development, create a better workforce, and drive global competitiveness. The emerging research on the long-term benefits of ECD, which shows widening payoffs in adulthood, gives conservatives an opening to revisit the issue and adjust their rhetoric.

Frankly, conservatives could steal the early childhood development issue and actually earn the title of compassionate conservatives, while changing the way we deliver welfare programs and measure their success—while also making us more globally competitive over the long term. However, they aren't going to get there by reducing benefits to distressed families, as many try to do now, and calling those families "entitled" or "takers." That talk reinforces conservatives' adherence to the mistaken premise about these families that poverty is "their fault" and "their problem" and that "they're just taking advantage of the system." And when a central premise is wrong, so are the supposed solutions that follow. It's time to wake up, read the research, reassess, and move forward.

Family stability, access to health care, good nutrition, and economic stability are all vital to SAFE and SANE settings for children. Conservatives are more likely to arrive at "ending poverty" by rethinking what we require of families in exchange for services. Instead of demanding menial work, as many programs do now, requiring adults to participate in early learning instruction and activities and positive engagement with their children makes a lot more sense in the long run.

A change in focus would enable conservatives to view support for social services through the lens of economic strength, global competitiveness, and ending the cycle of poverty through early childhood development. Such an approach would establish a common starting point with progressives in rethinking how to implement welfare programs.

While conservatives and progressives may have different reasons to support a child-focused welfare system (economic competitiveness versus social equity, to oversimply), the major goal of welfare for families with young children (promoting early childhood readiness to end poverty over the long term) could be shared by everyone. Everyone can fit in the tent. Wouldn't that be a nice change? Are we going to miss that opportunity, too?

Meanwhile, many other groups are missing opportunities in the arena of ECD:

An Important Role for Leaders in K-12 Education: *School leaders, especially superintendents,* should make early learning for children *before* they reach school age a high priority, because if it's implemented well in their district, it could rapidly accelerate improvement in school performance. Take a moment to dream about every third-grader in a school district achieving reading proficiency on time because their K–3 teachers could focus on teaching forward, rather than working backward on remedial tasks. Then dream of the graduation rates. Superintendents should be figuring out ways to make their staffing and budgets work to support birth-to-three efforts in their school districts and surrounding communities.

Visionary teachers, especially those in K–3, should have early learning high on their agenda. That they haven't established formal teams to crusade for early learning for ages zero through three is likely because they simply don't have the time and energy given their current workload, or, more accurately, overload. And that's because in most schools in distressed areas, teachers spend so much of their time on remedial teaching, helping the kids who are behind catch up with their peers. They are also swamped by paperwork and misdirected testing based on the wrong assumptions about why kids are failing. Hint (if you haven't figured it out by now): failure usually begins at home, not at school.

A Vital Role for Business Executives: *Business leaders* should jump quickly on the ECD bandwagon if they want a steady stream of good workers. If these leaders are the long-term strategic thinkers they are made out to be, they are not demonstrating it in most communities as it relates to early learning.

That most corporate leaders aren't on board with ECD also speaks to the quiet voices of its proponents, who haven't figured out how to engage their business community. This is another missed opportunity with huge negative consequences. Most existing early learning community coalitions have only one or two corporate leaders aggressively involved, if any. Come on, there are more visionary leaders in your business community than that. And several *will* become champions for early learning if recruited and given the opportunity.

Where Are the Media Thought Leaders? *Newspaper editorial boards and online opinion pages* should be leading on the issue of early childhood development, as every other social, educational, and economic issue covered as an editorial priority is potentially impacted by weak early learning systems. Advocating for strong early learning systems would help open the minds of others, particularly corporate and economic development leaders. Are editorial boards missing an opportunity to lead and inform on this issue?

Chambers of Commerce, Rotary Organizations, and Economic Development Boards Are Missing a Bet with Tepid Support of ECD: *Every economic development organization* should have ECD or early learning as the top issue on their agenda. Kids who are ready for school succeed in school. Kids who succeed in school graduate. Schools with great graduation rates attract outside business interests, because their employees want to live in communities with great schools. Communities with lots of young adults who are good workers also attract outside business. Creative cultures attract outside business. Bright young adults make us competitive on a worldwide basis. Yet very few economic development organizations have the key foundational issue of early learning anywhere on their radar, much less as a priority. It's an astounding misstep, another missed opportunity with huge negative consequences for a group that often prides itself on identifying and acting on opportunity.

Many economic development organizations think that finding a business to move into their area and giving it tax breaks to do so constitutes economic development (yes, that's oversimplified and doesn't give enough credit). Big thinkers in the economic development business know better. They know that attractive, successful schools; strong, talented workforces; vibrant downtowns and neighborhoods; strong, diverse communities; and lower crime rates are essential to recruiting outside businesses. The truly visionary economic development organizations are involved in all the key efforts to improve their schools, prepare a great workforce, and build a strong community infrastructure. Then their communities become legitimate business magnets.

The same can be said for Rotary organizations and chambers of commerce. Nowhere to be seen on most of their agendas is the fundamental community building block of early learning, perhaps one of the most important education, economic development, and ready-workforce issues of our time. Oops.

ECD as a Secret Weapon for More Rapid Advancement Among Children in Communities of Color: And while we're at it, where are *Urban League* organizations on the issue of early learning and ECD and family engagement and school readiness? Where are *Latino organizations, Native tribes, and immigrant-transition organizations*? Among many of their populations, unemployment and poverty are far higher than average, kids are living in high-stress environments, and many students don't complete high school. If we now know that early learning builds a strong foundation for later success in school and in life, these organizations should be among the strongest of advocates for early learning efforts in their communities. *They should also be actively administering such programs* or participating in collective impact coalitions to ensure that their approaches to early learning are culturally appropriate and effective. Are these groups active in the push to enhance ECD in your community? Is this a missed opportunity? Very likely.

ECD as a Business Advantage and Marketing Strategy for Childcare Providers: In some communities, organizations associated with early learning efforts are intimately involved with *childcare providers* to ensure movement toward higher-quality developmental care, especially for children ages zero through three. Some communities have implemented a quality-rating-and-improvement system in order to raise the bar for robust, research-based developmental efforts in childcare settings. Providers who can boast of highly rated developmental care can cement their business success by being on the "best provider" list.

How about your community? Are your childcare providers advocates for early learning and early childhood development? Are they participating in a program to improve quality of care?

The Need for More Aggressive Political Leadership Advocating for Advancing ECD Work: Where are your *mayors and city council members, your county executive and county council members, and your state legislators*? Sure, they don't want to get involved in "social services." It's "not their job." But the healthy economic development of your city and county and region is vitally important to them. Healthy schools are vital to them. Lower social service costs are important to them. And if that's the case, the fundamental building block upon which everything else rests should be vital to them, too. They should prioritize early learning, especially for ages zero through three, where long-term payoffs are greatest, and then the important transitional ECD stages of preschool, readiness for school, and achieving third-grade reading proficiency on time.

You: And finally, dear reader, **I come to you**. If you've come this far, you have likely picked up on the sense of urgency in this book. You might even be wondering, *What's the best thing I can do to help move early learning forward in my community?*

This could easily turn into one of the biggest contributions you'll make in your lifetime: helping children, families, and your community, maybe even your nation, move forward. Here's a quick synopsis of the book—facts that you should sear into your memory:

- People learn 60 to 80 percent of the knowledge they possess within the first three years of life. Starting very early with a strong foundation is critical to later success.
- If children are in a healthy setting, the resulting strong early brain development can serve them a lifetime.
- If children are in an unhealthy setting, it could cause them a lifetime of struggle and cost the rest of us a lot of money later in remedial services.

- Early childhood development (*before* school, with engaged caregivers) is key. Children who aren't ready for kindergarten or first grade will start behind and likely stay behind, and the gap widens more dramatically as teenagers move into young adulthood and later years.
- Around age ten, synapses and neurons that aren't "hardwired" into the brain through learning begin to atrophy—in a sense, to die. We are in a race with the best developmental timeline (very early), as well as the school-readiness timeline, to help create children who will be high performing in the long run and, as a result, be successful adults.
- SAFE and SANE settings are a key to successful early childhood brain development;
- Millions of children who need those settings do not have them;
- MOST communities have far to go to provide needed access to SAFE and SANE settings for children ages zero to three, not to mention growth and sustainability of those settings.
- Your nonprofit community likely already serves many distressed families, but how they coordinate on behalf of distressed children will vary widely from community to community and state to state.

With those facts at hand, how do you launch a comprehensive early learning effort in your community? First, it seems to me, you need to assess your community and learn who's doing what for families, especially distressed households where the risk of delayed childhood development is higher. Ask a few leaders of human-service nonprofit organizations for thirty minutes of their time to discuss what they do when they come face-to-face with families with young children, and more specifically what (if anything) they do to help provide SAFE and SANE settings for children. A few of these conversations with leaders in housing, nutrition, mental health, education, etc., should leave you with a good idea of whether there is an intentional, collaborative coalition in place to enhance early childhood development in your community. If you think it worthwhile, leave them each a copy of this book.

Second, ask about leadership on the specific issue of ECD. Who's providing it? Who's considered the most passionate and respected person on the issue? Then have a conversation with them. Ask them about the things they wish they had to advance the effort, but don't have. Ask if there's a way you can help them get those things.

Third, talk to a few friends who might want to accompany you on a few of these learning missions. Grow your circle of knowledgeable friends and associates.

Finally, when you've made connections and cultivated a small circle of interested friends, become an aggressive, passionate advocate. Reread the chapter on persuasion. Catch up with a nonprofit leader you've met and been impressed by, someone who would know how to leverage your knowledge and passion. Then go to work. Be bold.

The potential outcome is pretty darn good-looking. How about we all go to the prom together?

ACKNOWLEDGMENTS

There are so many participants in getting to this point . . . in writing and completing a book like this one . . . that it's difficult to acknowledge them all without writing a life history. In fact, if you've made it this far, you know that many of the stories that accompanied each chapter include real-life moments where others, unknowingly at the time, contributed to my ability to articulate the importance of early childhood development (ECD). So, first, to all those referenced in those moments in time, my sincere gratitude.

I want to also acknowledge a person not mentioned specifically in *Great by Eight* who probably, more than anyone else, accelerated my "deep dive" into ECD professional work, both research and program development. When I started in the mid-1980s with Pierce County Community Action, much of the work focused on assisting families in distress. My boss, Tom Hilyard, the director of Human Services for the county, immediately tasked me with bringing Washington State's just-being-developed Early Childhood Education and Assistance Program (ECEAP) into the county. At the time, the county had nearly 800,000 people and a single Head Start program barely scratching the surface of the many children and families who could benefit. He gave me support, encouragement, and a very long leash in building a robust ECEAP presence. Tom's vision and steadfast support for that new ECEAP venture is responsible, as much as anyone or anything, for all that evolved in early childhood work in Pierce County after that initial challenge.

As *Great by Eight* also made clear, establishing a sustained commitment to a functioning ECD effort takes many partners willing to take leaps of faith into territory not traditionally well funded over the long term. To my fun and fantastic staff at Community Action, to my "other organization" colleagues in our early Prevention Partnership for Children, and to my deeply committed staff and Board of Directors at United Way of Pierce County, thank you. You all challenged me to accompany my enthusiasm with realistic thinking about our potential role in ECD; then, you dared to explore new ground because it was the right thing to do despite the risks. A big shout-out also to my colleagues at United Way organizations throughout Washington State, who made the bold choice to make ECD a priority in statewide advocacy, and brought important help to many underserved children, families, and communities. To all of you, your unwavering commitment to the betterment of our larger community was and is a constant inspiration.

In equal measure, my gratitude goes to the many nonprofit organizations and their leaders who were doing yeoman's work with distressed families before I ever arrived, often doing so on a shoestring of constantly fluctuating funding . . . but many of whom nevertheless proved willing to consider taking on additional ECD tasks; I was clumsy at times in articulating how many of them might play a contributing part within their own areas of expertise, but our ongoing discussions, some of them admittedly difficult, helped bring clarity to how we might partner, and helped bring ECD into a more visible and effective place in the community. What these nonprofit leaders continue to accomplish in constantly challenging circumstances is a tremendous story in its own right.

As for the more technical aspect of making this book at least somewhat coherent, my appreciation to Dr. Jeremy Stringer and to Marion Woyvodich, both of whom gave freely of their time and talent in the initial effort to organize, edit, and make sense of *Great by Eight*. It was their second time daring to take on the initial in-depth review of a book of mine, and their assistance once again proved invaluable.

Many other good friends and family members gave me feedback on the content and the cover design and actually helped with financial contributions to get *Great by Eight* off the ground. Their confidence and trust drove me to persevere.

And of course, once again the staff at Girl Friday Productions shone through with their multiple and exceptional talents. They have a long and impressive history of helping independent authors publish impressive books. Sara Spees Addicott as senior editor for Book Development, Bethany Davis as editorial production manager, Paul Barrett as art director (outstanding book cover designs for this and a different book, *Inside Pitch*), Allison Gorman, copyeditor, who somehow from afar was able to read my mind and bring power and clarity throughout, and Monique Vescia, proofreader, all contributed to making the journey productive, professional, and actually pleasurable . . . no small feat in this business.

And to my younger siblings, John, Rob, and Jonelle. They shared with me an early lifetime of ups and downs, both environments explored in *Great by Eight* . . . a great mom and dad suddenly impacted by the severe mental illness of our father; this, followed by living on the edge of poverty; a single mom forced to start over with four children in the 1950s; then a marriage, partly driven by desperation, that devolved into years of an alcoholic stepfather's mental and physical abuse. Especially at a critical time in the lives of my younger brothers and sister, life included the nightmare of extreme and constant stress so many other families also face. But we hung together. We shared the early experience of a loving extended family, at times living with each set of grandparents; and we protected and cared for one another. As a result, we survived the bad times. Each of us is a mentally strong, healthy, and successful adult. I was as amazed by their resilience then as I am proud of their successful and happy lives now. And, I am thankful for their constant love and support, which meant so much then and sustains me even today.

Finally, to my grandchildren Phoenix, Scarlett, Isla, and Eva, who have just passed through or are living now through those important early years, remember: Grandpa (and Grammy) have a secret.

NOTES

INTRODUCTION

1   David Alexander, "Leading for Kids," email message to subscribers (September 2020).

CHAPTER 1

2   "Why Early Childhood Matters: Brain Development," First Things First (accessed November 14, 2020), http://www.firstthingsfirst.org/early-childhood-matters/braindevelopment/#:~: text=And%20early%20brain%20development%20has,shape%20how%20their%20brain%20 develops.

3   Christopher Bergland, "Tackling the 'Vocabulary Gap' Between Rich and Poor Children," *The Athletes Way* (blog), in *Psychology Today* (February 16, 2014), http://www.psychologytoday. com/us/blog/the-athletes-way/201402/tackling-the-vocabulary-gap-between-rich-and-poor -children?amp.

4   T. R. Risley and B. Hart, "Promoting Early Language Development," *Child psychology and mental health. The crisis in youth mental health: Critical issues and effective programs*, vol. 4 (2006), http://psycnet.apa.org/record/2006-02299-004.

5   T. R. Risley and B. Hart, "Closing the Achievement Gap with Baby Talk," *Morning Edition*, NPR (January 10, 2011), http://www.npr.org/2011/01/10/132740565/closing-the-achievement-gap -with-baby-talk.

6   Fernald, Anne, Bjorn Carey, et.al., "Language Gap Between Rich and Poor Children Begins in Infancy, Stanford Psychologists Find," *Stanford News Service* (September 25, 2013), http://news .stanford.edu/pr/2013/pr-toddler-language-gap-091213.html.

CHAPTER 2

7   Child Poverty, National Center for Children in Poverty (website), https://stage.nccp.org/topics /childpoverty.html.

8   David Alexander and Mark Weitecha, "A Wake-up Call: Boomers, Babies and the Future of the U.S.: The Economic Case for Investing in Children," Lucile Packard Foundation for Children's Health and Children's Hospital Association (website), July 2017.

CHAPTER 3

9   Editorial Board, "The Ivanka Entitlement," *The Wall Street Journal* (May 25, 2017), The Ivanka Entitlement - WSJ.

10 Maggie Mallon, "Ivanka Trump's Paid Family Leave Plan Neglects One Major Thing," *Glamour* (July 5, 2017), http://www.glamour.com/story/ivank-trump-paid-family-leave-plan.

11 Prachi Gupta, "Ivanka Trump on Her Father's New Child Care and Maternity Leave Policy," *Cosmopolitan* (September 14, 2016), http://www.cosmopolitan.com/politics/a3356886/ivanka-trump-child-care-maternity-leave-policy/.

CHAPTER 4

12 Juliana Herman, Sasha Post, and Scott O'Halloran, "Infographic: We're Getting Beat on Preschool," Center for American Progress, Education K-12 (website) (May 2, 2013), http://www.americanprogress.org/issues/education-k-12/news/2013/05/02/62048/infographic-were-getting-beat-on-preschool/.

CHAPTER 5

13 "Adverse Childhood Experiences (ACES)," Joining Forces for Children (website), http://www.joiningforcesforchildren.org/what-are-aces.

14 David Alexander and Mark Weitecha, "A Wake-up Call: Boomers, Babies and the Future of the U.S.: The Economic Case for Investing in Children," Lucile Packard Foundation for Children's Health and Children's Hospital Association (website) (July 2017).

CHAPTER 6

15 "High Return on Investment (ROI)," The Center for High Impact Philanthropy, School of Social Policy and Practice, University of Pennsylvania (website) (2020), http://www.impact.upenn.edu/early-childhood-toolkit/why-invest/what-is-the-return-on-investment/. "Nurturing Care for Early Childhood Development," World Health Organization (May 18, 2018), http://www.who.int/maternal_child_adolescent/child/nurturing-care-framework/en/. "Evidence for ECD Investment," UNICEF for Every Child (July 16, 2013), http://www.unicef.org/earlychildhood/index_69851.html.

16 Kayt Sukel, "The Young and the Riskless," *Discover* (July 27, 2016).

17 Kayt Sukel, "The Young and the Riskless," *Discover* (July 27, 2016).

18 Kayt Sukel, "The Young and the Riskless," *Discover* (July 27, 2016).

19 David Alexander and Mark Weitecha, "A Wake-up Call: Boomers, Babies and the Future of the U.S.: The Economic Case for Investing in Children," Lucile Packard Foundation for Children's Health and Children's Hospital Association (website) (July 2017).

20 "Despite World's Largest Economy, U.S. Ranks Ninth in Child Prosperity; Germany Ranks First," Save the Children (website) (July 22, 2016), http://www.savethechildren.org/us/about-us /media-and-news/2016-press-releases/despite-world---s-largest-economy--u-s--ranks-ninth -on-child-pro.

CHAPTER 8

21 *The Ellen DeGeneres Show,* "Adorable 3-Year-Old Periodic Table Expert Brielle," YouTube (November 23, 2015), http://www.bing.com/videos/search?q=you+tube+brielle+tables&docid =608042257198287125&mid=690493352A5544CB787E690493352A5544CB787E&view =detail&FORM=VIRE.

22 Eun Kyung Kim, "Little Girl Recalls Periodic Table Elements for Ellen DeGeneres, Blows Our Minds," *Today* (November 24, 2015), http://www.today.com/parents/little-girl-recalls-periodic -table-elements-ellen-degeneres-blows-our-t57791.

CHAPTER 9

23 Allan Akhtar, Drake Baer, and Rachel Gillet, "25 Ways Your Childhood Impacts How Successful You Become as an Adult," OME Careers, Business Insider (August 19, 2015), http://www .businessinsider.com/how-your-childhood-affects-your-success.

24 Neil Petersen, "How Behavior in Kindergarten Can Predict Later Success," AllPsych (website) (August 27, 2015), http://blog.allpsych.com/how-behavior-in-kindergarten-can-predict-later -success/.

25 Cherylann Bellavia, "When to Start Music Lessons," Children's Music Workshop, National Educational Music Company, http://www.nemc.com/resources/articles/when-to-start -lessons_44.

26 "The Best Time to Learn a Foreign Language," NBC News (July 20, 2009), Unraveling how kids become bilingual so easily (nbcnews.com).

27 "The Best Time to Learn a Foreign Language," NBC News (July 20, 2009), Unraveling how kids become bilingual so easily (nbcnews.com).

28 "Early Childhood Mathematics: Promoting Good Beginnings," the National Association for the Education of Young Children (NAEYC) and the National Council for Teachers of Mathematics (NCTM), http://www.state.nj.us/education/ece/pd/math/naeyc_nctm.pdf.

29 D. H. Clements, Conference Working Group, "Early Childhood Mathematics," http://www .bing.com/search?q=Clements%2C%20D.%20H.%2C%20%26%20Conference%20Working%20 Group.%20(2004).%20Part%201%3A%20Major%20themes%20and%20recommendation.

30 Kristin Stanberry, "Early Math Matters: Preparing Preschoolers to Succeed," Get Ready to Read (website), http://www.getreadytoread.org/early-learning-childhood-basics/early-math /early-math-matters-preparing-preschoolers-to-succeed.

31 Lisa Guernsey, "Learning to Read: How Young is Too Young," *HuffPost* (July 12, 2011), http:// www.huffpost.com/entry/learning-to-read-how-youn_b_860964.

32 Kate Shaw Yoshida, "Getting Kids on the Right Track with Early Science Education," *ARS Technica* (August 21, 2011), http://arstechnica.com/science/2011/08/getting-kids-on-the-right-track-with-early-science-education/.

33 Joshua M. Sneideman, "Engaging Children in STEM Education EARLY!" Natural Start Alliance (December 2013), http://naturalstart.org/feature-stories/engaging-children-stem-education-early.

34 Damon E. Jones, Mark Greenberg, and Max Crowley, "Early Social-Emotional Functioning and Public Health: The Relationship Between Kindergarten Social Competence and Future Wellness," *American Journal of Public Health* (November 2015), http://ajph.aphapublications.org/doi/full/10.2105/AJPH.2015.302630.

35 Penny Bauder, "Teach STEM Education with Nature Exploration," Green Kids Crafts (website) (June 3, 2019), http://www.greenkidcrafts.com/teach-stem-education-with-nature-exploration/.

CHAPTER 10

36 Damon E. Jones, Mark Greenberg, and Max Crowley, "Early Social-Emotional Functioning and Public Health: The Relationship Between Kindergarten Social Competence and Future Wellness," *American Journal of Public Health* (November 2015), http://ajph.aphapublications.org/doi/full/10.2105/AJPH.2015.302630.

CHAPTER 11

37 Charlotte Alter, "Black Children Still Most Likely to Live in Poverty, Study Says," *Time* (July 14, 2015), http://time.com/3955671/black-children-poverty-study/.

38 Andrew J. Friedenthal, "The Toys That Played Us," *Sightlines* (February 11, 2018), http://webcache.googleusercontent.com/search?q=cache:7Sl2Im4exAcJ:https://sightlinesmag.org/toys-played-us+&cd=1&hl=en&ct=clnk&gl=us.

39 Ashley Crossman, "Malcolm Gladwell's *The Tipping Point*," *ThoughtCo*, http://www.thoughtco.com/malcolm-gladwell-tipping-point-theory-3026765.

40 Gina Heeb, "US Income Inequality Jumps to Highest Level Ever Recorded," *Business Insider* (September 27, 2019).

CHAPTER 14

41 Alex Crippen, "Warren Buffett's Nine Essential Rules for Running a Business," CNBC (November 21, 2016), http://www.cnbc.com/2016/11/21/warren-buffett-9-essential-rules-for-running-a-business.html.

42 Venkata Sreekanth Sampath, "The Qualities That Make Warren Buffett the Man He Is," *The Tao of Wealth, Business, Investing, and Finance* (October 28, 2015), http://thetaoofwealth

.wordpress.com/2015/10/28/the-qualities-that-make-warren-buffett-the-man-he-is/.

CHAPTER 15

43 Libby Doggett and Albert Wat, "Pre-K in American Cities," City Health, An Initiative of the Beaumont Foundation and Kaiser Permanente, partnered with the National Institute for Early Education Research, http://www.debeaumont.org/wp-content/uploads/2019/04/Pre-KinAmericanCities1-23.pdf.

CHAPTER 16

44 Marshall Barer, composer. *Mighty Mouse Theme Song and Farmer Alfalfa Song.* Originally released in 1962.

CHAPTER 19

45 Tamara G. Halle and Kristen E. Darling-Churchill, "Review of Measures of Social and Emotional Development," *Journal of Applied Developmental Psychology* (March 2016), http://www.researchgate.net/publication/297718407_Review_of_measures_of_social_and_emotional_development.
46 Nicholas Kristof, "Too Small to Fail," *New York Times* (June 2, 2016), http://www.nytimes.com/2016/06/02/opinion/building-childrens-brains.html.
47 Mark D'Alessio, "The Best and Worst States for Early Childhood Education," Center for Education and Workforce, U.S. Chamber of Commerce Foundation (January 7, 2015), http://www.uschamberfoundation.org/blog/post/best-and-worst-states-early-childhood-education/42427.

CHAPTER 20

48 Linda Jacobson, "Report: Overall Pre-K Spending Grows, but Few States Make Gains in Quality, Enrollment," National Institute for Early Education Research (April 17, 2019), http://www.educationdive.com/news/report-overall-pre-k-spending-grows-but-few-states-make-gains-in-quality/552803/.
49 John Kania and Mark Kramer, "Collective Impact," *Stanford Social Innovation Review* (Winter 2011), http://ssir.org/articles/entry/collective_impact#.
50 Fay Hanleybrown, John Kania, and Mark Kramer, "Channeling Change: Making Collective Impact Work," *Stanford Social Innovation Review* (January 26, 2012), http://ssir.org/articles/entry/channeling_change_making_collective_impact_work.
51 Valerie Bockstette, "Early Wins in Early Childhood: A Case Study in Seeding Systems Change," FSG, http://www.fsg.org/publications/early-wins-early-childhood.
52 Fay Hanleybrown, John Kania, and Mark Kramer, "Channeling Change: Making Collective

Impact Work," *Stanford Social Innovation Review* (January 26, 2012), http://ssir.org/articles /entry/channeling_change_making_collective_impact_work.

53 Fay Hanleybrown, John Kania, and Mark Kramer, "Channeling Change: Making Collective Impact Work," *Stanford Social Innovation Review* (January 26, 2012), http://ssir.org/articles /entry/channeling_change_making_collective_impact_work.

54 Fay Hanleybrown, John Kania, and Mark Kramer, "Channeling Change: Making Collective Impact Work," *Stanford Social Innovation Review* (January 26, 2012), http://ssir.org/articles /entry/channeling_change_making_collective_impact_work.

CHAPTER 21

55 H. Luke Shaefer and Kathryn Edin, "Extreme Poverty in the United States, 1996 to 2011," University of Michigan National Poverty Center (2011), http://policybrief28.pdf (umich.edu).

56 Belinda Luscombe, "How Family Breakfasts Became the New Family Dinner," *Time* (September 5, 2019), http://time.com/5669532/family-meal-breakfast/.

57 Belinda Luscombe, "How Family Breakfasts Became the New Family Dinner," *Time* (September 5, 2019), http://time.com/5669532/family-meal-breakfast/.

Beth Babcock, "Using Brain Science to Design New Pathways Out of Poverty," EMPath (Economic Mobility Pathways) (January 2014), http://www.empathways.org/research-policy/publications.

58 Beth Babcock, "Using Brain Science to Design New Pathways Out of Poverty," EMPath (Economic Mobility Pathways) (January 2014), http://www.empathways.org/research-policy /publications.

59 Tara García Mathewson, "How Poverty Changes the Brain," *The Atlantic* (April 19, 2017), http://www.theatlantic.com/education/archive/2017/04/can-brain-science-pull-families-out -of-poverty/523479/.

60 Beth Babcock, "Using Brain Science to Design New Pathways Out of Poverty," EMPath (Economic Mobility Pathways) (January 2014), http://www.empathways.org/research-policy /publications.

ABOUT THE AUTHOR

Dr. Rick Allen was named in 2001 one of the first Business Leaders of the Year in Pierce County, Washington, by the University of Washington Tacoma School of Business in association with the Business Examiner News Group. Allen was also recognized by the Washington Association for the Education of Young Children as one of the state's outstanding community-based advocates for children.

Allen worked in the nonprofit field as president and CEO of United Way of Pierce County, Washington, a community approaching one million, for more than twenty years. Before that he served eight years as director of the Pierce County Community Action Agency, working predominantly with families in distress.

He served on the task force to assist in the development of the curriculum for Seattle University's Master of Nonprofit Leadership program.

He was twice chosen by his peers to be president of statewide associations, United Ways of Washington and the Washington State Community Action Association. During his tenures, both statewide organizations focused on helping their local members advocate more effectively at the community level and collectively at the state level. He had earlier been selected by the National Community Action Foundation for a congressional lobbying internship in Washington, D.C.

Often humorously referred to as "the godfather of early learning" in Pierce County, Allen was also a leading advocate for the aggressive expansion of community-based non-profit early childhood development programs statewide. He was frequently asked to testify on the subject before the Washington State Legislature. The successful community collaboration he was instrumental in helping establish in Pierce County remains active today, as do many of the early childhood efforts in other Washington State communities.

While with the Pierce County Community Action, Allen and his team started up and administered a number of the first Early Childhood Education and Assistance Programs in Pierce County and Washington State, and helped expand Head Start and Early Head Start programs in Pierce County, as well.

During the same period, Allen served as the chair of a Washington State citizen advisory committee on welfare reform, the Family Independence Program. As chair, he traveled across the state to meet and learn from families in economic distress, as well as with state staff workers assigned to assist those families.

Allen's Community Action team won a national Housing and Urban Development award for an innovative welfare-to-work design. The HUD award resulted in Allen's participation in a presentation in Washington, D.C., with the vice president of the United States as moderator. Ideas developed in the design were later incorporated into Washington State's welfare programs.

Allen holds a bachelor's degree in journalism from Eastern Washington University, a master's degree in interpersonal communication from Ohio University, and both a master's and a doctorate in public administration from the University of Southern California. His history also includes diverse experiences that have enhanced his understanding of what he calls "different worlds and values." Here are just a few:

- *Working his way through college, Allen baled hay on an eastern Washington farm; worked as a dishwasher and night janitor at a large restaurant; laid railroad track in central Oregon (as a "gandy dancer"); and worked construction in Pullman, Washington.*

- *In college, he was a residence hall assistant (RA), was later elected student body vice president, and was named one of the Top Ten Seniors in his college graduating class.*
- *During the Vietnam era, he was a captain in the US Army Infantry (Airborne).*
- *He has eleven years in higher education administration, including a term as Vice President and Dean of Student Life at Pacific Lutheran University.*
- *During the development and start-up of the Washington State Housing Finance Commission, he was manager of Washington State Housing Programs.*
- *He is the founder and previous owner of two small businesses. One was art related, and the other a wine shop he helped start up with his brother John who now has the oldest and largest wine club in the Pacific Northwest.*
- *He is the author of a book about Major League Baseball,* Inside Pitch: Insiders Reveal How the Ill-Fated Seattle Pilots Got Played into Bankruptcy in One Year.

CPSIA information can be obtained
at www.ICGtesting.com
Printed in the USA
FSHW020254240421
80621FS

9 781734 595925